Microsoft®

POWERPOINT 2000

Copyright - Editions ENI - May 2000
ISBN: 2-7460-0793-2
Original edition: ISBN: 2-7460-0672-3

ENI Publishing LTD

500 Chiswick High Road
London W4 5RG

Tel: 020 8956 2320
Fax: 020 8956 2321

e-mail: publishing@ediENI.com
http://www.publishing-eni.com

Editions ENI

BP 32125
44021 NANTES Cedex 1

Tel : 33 02 40 92 45 45
Fax : 33 02 40 92 45 46

e-mail : editions@ediENI.com
http://www.editions-eni.com

Straight to the point collection directed by Corinne HERVO

Foreword

The aim of this book is to let you find rapidly how to perform any task in the presentation software **PowerPoint 2000**.

Each procedure is described in detail and illustrated so that you can put it into action easily.

The final pages are given over to an **index** of the topics covered and a set of **appendices**, which give details of shortcut keys and toolbars.

The typographic conventions used in this book are as follows:

Type faces used for specific purposes:	
bold	indicates the option to take in a menu or dialog box.
italic	is used for notes and comments.
Ctrl	represents a key from the keyboard; when two keys appear side by side, they should be pressed simultaneously.

Symbols indicating the content of a paragraph:	
▓	an action to carry out (activating an option, clicking with the mouse...).
⇨	a general comment on the command in question.
⌐🖰	a technique which involves the mouse.
⟨⬦⟩	a keyboard technique.

📖 OVERVIEW

📖 PRINTING

📖 DOCUMENTS

📖 SLIDE SHOWS

📖 SLIDES

📖 TEXT

7️⃣ OBJECTS

8️⃣ CHARTS

9️⃣ MACROS

🔟 INTERNET/INTRANET

APPENDIX

INDEX

1.1 The environment

A-Starting/leaving PowerPoint

▓ Click the **Start** button on the taskbar, point to the **Programs** option and click the **Microsoft PowerPoint** option.

▓ The first time you start PowerPoint, the Office Assistant appears: choose to **Start using Microsoft PowerPoint**.

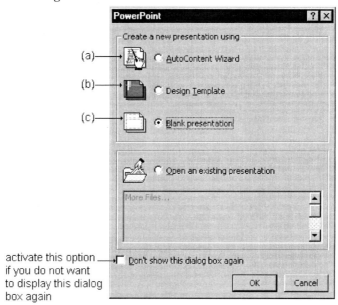

(a) The wizard that comes with the AutoContent Wizard option
(b) Design Template
(c) Blank presentation

Open an existing presentation

activate this option if you do not want to display this dialog box again — Don't show this dialog box again

▓ Choose to **Create a new presentation** or **Open an existing presentation**.

(a) The wizard guides you step by step through the creation procedure.

(b) This option gives you a choice of templates.

(c) This option creates a blank presentation.

▓ To leave PowerPoint:

| **File** | Click the button | Alt F4 |
| **Exit** | in the application window | |

▓ If necessary, save any modifications which have been made since the last time the open documents were saved.

B-The working environment

░ The PowerPoint environment includes two types of window: the application window and the presentation window.

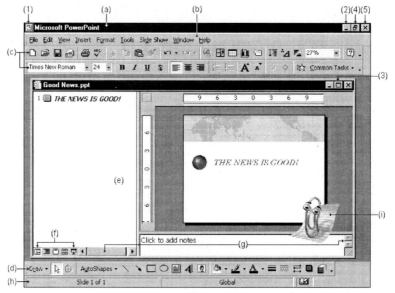

(a) The title bar, which contains the Control menu button (1), the Minimize (2), Maximize (3) (or Restore (4)) buttons and the Close button (5).

(b) The menu bar, which includes a **Help** menu.

(c) (d) The toolbars which appear on screen depend on choices made during the previous session.

(e) The workspace, made up to three panes (Outlines, Slide and Notes Page).

(f) PowerPoint's five views.

(g) The scroll bars.

(h) The status bar.

(i) The Office Assistant.

C-Using the menus

░ PowerPoint's menus are variable. When you start to use PowerPoint, the menus display only the most popular commands, and then adapt to your usage and display the commands you use the most.

░ To see an entire menu, point to the double-headed black arrow at the bottom of the menu, or click the menu and wait for 5 seconds.

░ To see a shortcut menu, point to the item for which you want to see a shortcut menu and click the right mouse button. To close a shortcut menu without choosing any of the commands, press Esc.

⇨ *To see full menus all the time, deactivate the **Menus show recently used commands first** option in the **Options** tab of the **Tools - Customize** dialog box.*

D-Using the Office Assistant

▦ To display the Office Assistant click the 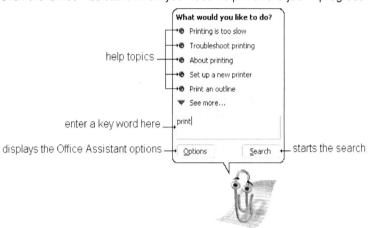 button or use **Help - Show the Office Assistant**.

▦ Click the Office Assistant when you need help with the job in progress.

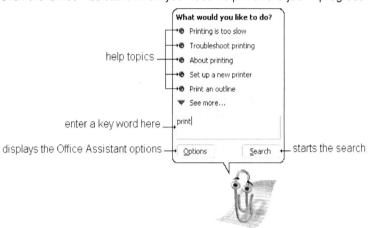

When the Office Assistant has some advice for you, it displays a light bulb. Click the Assistant to read the advice.

▦ To change the look of the Office Assistant, click the **Options** button in the Office Assistant window then activate the **Gallery** tab.

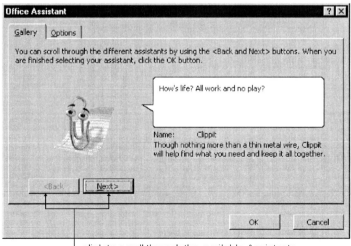

E-Using PowerPoint's help

▦ Deactivate the Office Assistant: click the Assistant then the **Options** button. In the **Options** tab, deactivate **Use the Office Assistant** and confirm with **OK**.

▦ **Help - Microsoft PowerPoint Help**

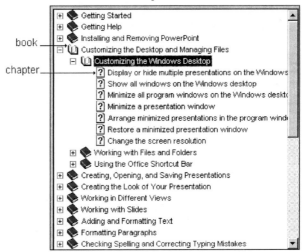

▦ To use the Contents page to find help on a particular topic, click the **Contents** tab, double-click a book then a chapter.

▦ If you want to ask a question, click the **Answer Wizard** tab.

▦ To use the index to search for a topic, click the **Index** tab.
Indicate the topic you are looking for: type in a key word or the first few characters of a key word and/or select a topic from the list.

⇨ *If you activate* **Help - What's This?** *(or press* 🔲Shift 🔲F1 *) and then click an object on the screen, PowerPoint provides a description of the object.*

F-Undoing the last actions

▦ To undo your last action, use:

Edit   🔄   Ctrl **Z**
Undo

▦ To undo several of your last actions, open the 🔄▾ list.

▨ Click the earliest of the actions you want to undo (the one which appears furthest down the list). PowerPoint undoes all the actions which are selected in the list.

▨ To restore the last action(s) that you undid, click .

⇨ *By default, you can undo up to 20 actions. You can change this number using* **Tools - Options, Edit** *tab,* **Maximum number of undos** *text box.*

⇨ *To repeat your last action, use* **Edit - Redo** *or* ⌨Ctrl **Y**.

1.2 Viewing objects in the window

A-Changing the view

*As you create and structure a presentation, you can use the four different views, which are accessible via buttons at the bottom of the window (*Notes Page *view can be accessed by the* View *menu):*

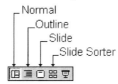

The three views Normal, Outline and Slide are made up of three resizable panes: the Outline pane, Slide pane and Notes pane.

▨ **Slide Sorter** view:

View
Slide Sorter

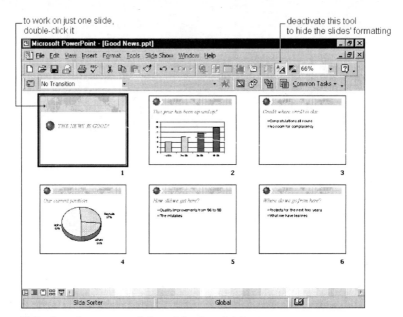

This view shows you all the slides in miniature.

Normal view:

View
Normal

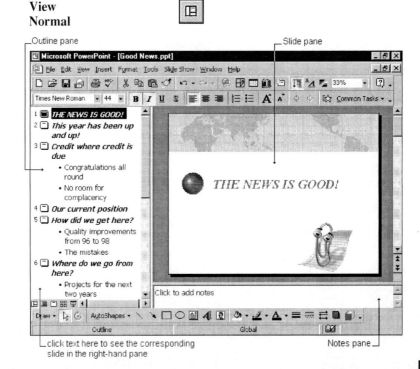

This view allows you to see the slide contents and the presentation outline.

- **Outline** view:

Click the [button] button in the bottom left corner of the window.

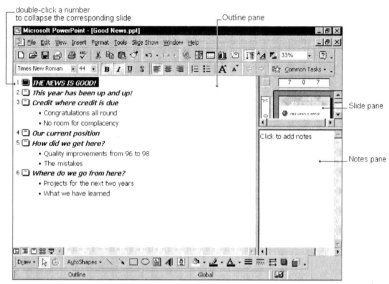

This view lets you see the titles and textual content of the presentation. It is a quick way of creating and organising a presentation.

- **Slide** view:

Click the [button] button in the bottom left corner of the window.

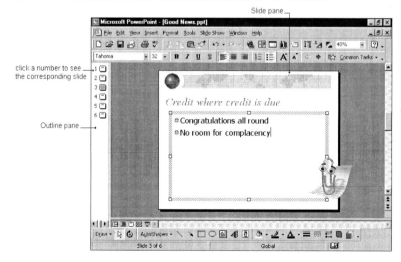

This view shows the slide in a larger pane. One slide appears on the screen at a time.

▓ **Notes Page** view:

View
Notes Page

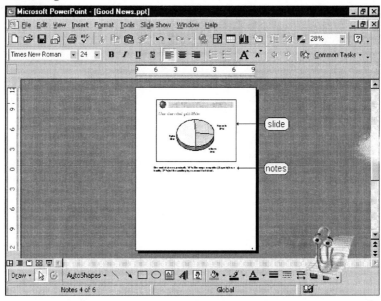

Activate this view to enter notes concerning the content of a slide.

⇨ *The current view is shown on the Status bar.*

B-Changing the zoom

▓ Open the `26%` list box on the **Standard** toolbar.

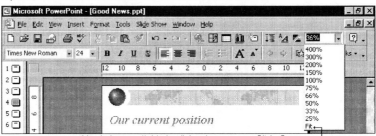

this choice, available in all the views except Slide Sorter,
allows you to see the whole slide/page

▓ Choose one of the values in the list or type in your own value and press `Enter` .

⇨ *You can also use the* **View - Zoom** *command to change the magnification.*

C-Displaying/hiding the rulers/the guides

▓ In the **View** menu, activate or deactivate the corresponding options.

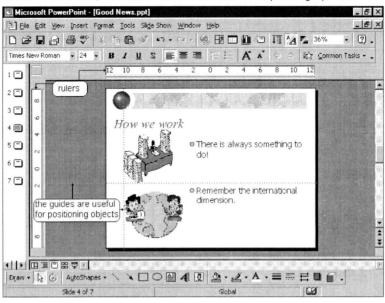

⇨ *You can reposition the guides by dragging them.*

⇨ *If the vertical ruler does not appear, use **Tools - Options**, activate the* ***View*** *tab and activate the **Vertical ruler** option.*

D-Displaying/hiding toolbars

▓ Right-click one of the toolbars.

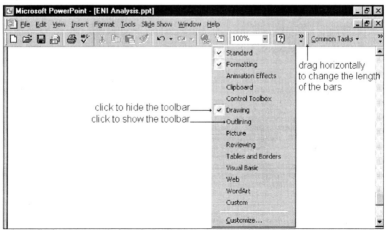

Some bars can be shown/hidden by clicking a tool:

 Tables and Borders toolbar

 Animation Effects toolbar

 3D Settings toolbar

To float a toolbar, drag its move handle to its new position. The toolbar now has a title bar and a ⊠ button. Dock a floating toolbar by double-clicking its title bar.

E-Customising a toolbar

Modifying a toolbar

Tools - Customize

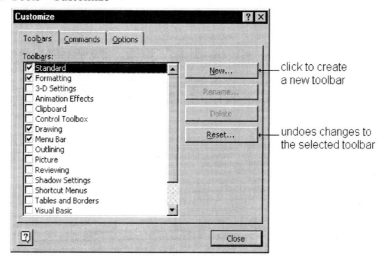

Make sure that the toolbar you want to modify is displayed by clicking the corresponding box in the **Toolbars** list.

To delete a button from one of the toolbars in the window, drag the button off the toolbar in the window.

To move a button, drag the button along the toolbar until it reaches its new position. To copy a button, hold down the Ctrl key as you drag.

To edit the ScreenTip associated with a button, right-click the button concerned, enter the text of the ScreenTip in the **Name** box, then press Enter .

Adding a tool

░ Tools - Customize

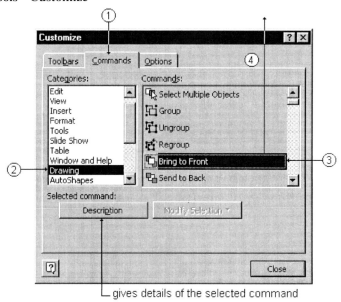

gives details of the selected command

① Activate this tab.

② Select the category containing the command that you want to add to the toolbar.

③ Select the command.

④ Drag the command to the position on the toolbar where you want the button to appear.

⇨ *The **Add or Remove Buttons** option, accessible by clicking* ⬛ *(or* ⬛*) can also be used to add or remove buttons on a toolbar.*

2.1 Printing a presentation

A-Printing a presentation

▓ Select the slides to be printed; if all the slides are to be printed, you do not need to select them.

▓ **File - Print** or Ctrl **P**

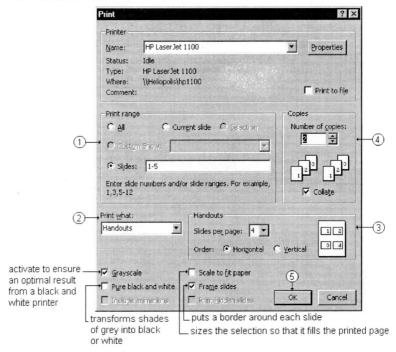

activate to ensure an optimal result from a black and white printer

└ transforms shades of grey into black or white

└ puts a border around each slide
└ sizes the selection so that it fills the printed page

① Indicate which slides are to be printed.

② Specify what to print: **Slides, Handouts**.

③ Indicate the number of slides per page and the print order.

④ Specify how many copies to print. If you are printing several copies, activate **Collate** to print the first copy of the entire document before starting on the next.

⑤ Start printing.

⇨ *By default, slides are printed with a Landscape orientation. The default scale is 24 cm by 18 cm.*

⇨ *The* 🖨 *button on the standard toolbar prints instantly without displaying the dialog box. It applies the last options set.*

B-Printing notes pages or an outline

▥ **File - Print** or Ctrl **P**

▥ Open the **Print what** list and choose **Notes Pages** or **Outline View**.

▥ Click **OK** to start printing.

⇨ *When you print notes pages, they are numbered automatically. The numbers of the pages correspond to the numbers of the slides.*

⇨ *You can customize the printing of Notes pages by changing the Notes Master (View - Master).*

2.2 Page setup

A-Modifying the page setup for printing slides

▥ **File - Page Setup**

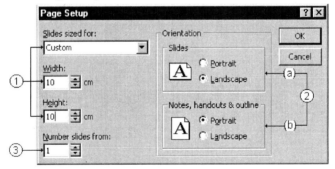

① Choose one of the standard sizes, or specify the width and height of the printed slides.

② Choose the orientation of the paper for printing slides (a) and/or for printing notes, handouts or the outline (b).

③ Give the number to print on the first slide.

B-Customising your handouts

▒ View - Master - Handout Master

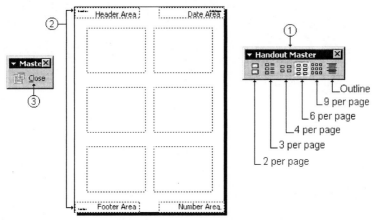

① Indicate the layout, which will apply to all the pages of the document.

② Define the header, the footer and any other item which is going to appear on all the pages.

③ Return to the previous view.

▒ When you want to print the handouts, open the **Print** dialog box and, from the **Print what** list, select **Handouts** then the layout that you have customised (2, 3, 4, 6 or 9 slides per page).

⇨ *The quickest way to access the handout master is to hold down the* ⎡û Shift⎤ *key as you click* 🔳 *or* 🔳 *.*

3.1 Presentations

A document created in PowerPoint is called a presentation.

A-Opening a presentation

░ **File**　　　　　　　

　　Open

① Select the drive and the folder where the document is stored.

② Double-click the name of the document to open.

⇨ *To reopen one of the last four presentations used, open the **File** menu, then click the presentation's name, which appears at the bottom of the menu.*

B-Closing a presentation

░ **File**　　　　　　 Click the ☒ button

　　Close　　　　　 in the document window

░ Save your changes if necessary.

C-Creating a presentation

▓ File - New

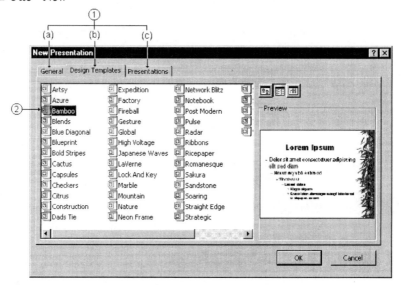

① Open the page which contains the template you require:

(a)   to use the Blank Presentation template or one that you have created yourself.

(b)   to choose one of PowerPoint's templates.

(c)   to select one of the PowerPoint templates which includes a certain amount of text.

② Double-click the name of the template.

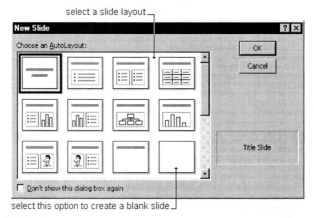

⇨ *The* 🖺 *tool creates a new document based on the **Blank Presentation** template.*

D-Saving a presentation

A new presentation

File   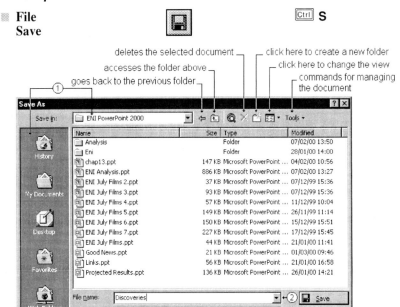   Ctrl S
Save

deletes the selected document — ⌐ click here to create a new folder
accesses the folder above — ⌐ click here to change the view
goes back to the previous folder — ⌐ commands for managing
the document

① Select the drive and folder in which to save the document.

② Give a name for the new document (up to 255 characters long, spaces included).

An existing presentation

File   Ctrl S
Save

⇨ *PowerPoint presentations have the extension PPT.*

⇨ *The command **File - Save As** can be used to save a duplicate of the presentation under a different name.*

⇨ *To allow PowerPoint to recover a reasonably up-to-date version of the document if, for example, the computer shuts down suddenly, go into the **Tool - Options** dialog box, open the **Save** page, activate the **Save Auto-Recover info every** option then give the interval between automatic saves.*

⇨ *To define the default folder, activate the **Save** tab in the **Options** dialog box (**Tools - Options**) and give the name and location of the folder in **Default file location**.*

E-Going to a presentation that is open but hidden

▒ Click the corresponding button on the taskbar or select the presentation in the **Window** menu:

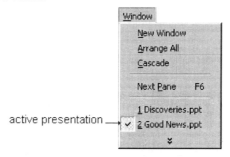

active presentation ⟶

F-Inserting one presentation inside another

▒ Activate the slide where you want to insert the presentation.

▒ Use the **Insert - Object** command or, if the slide includes a placeholder for an inserted object, double-click it.

activate this option if the inserted
presentation might be modified later
and you want any changes to be
updated in the current presentation

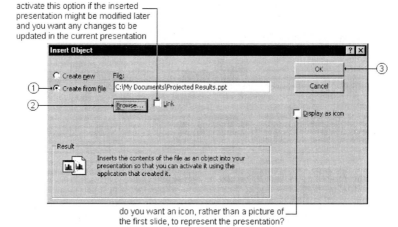

do you want an icon, rather than a picture of
the first slide, to represent the presentation?

① Activate this option.

② Click here and select the name of the presentation to insert.

③ Insert the presentation.

⇨ *To edit the source of the inserted presentation, select the icon or the picture which represents it and use **Edit - Presentation Object - Open**. Edit the original document and return to the destination presentation by **File - Close & Return to**.*

⇨ *To run the slide show of the inserted presentation (in Slide view of the host presentation but not during the slide show) double-click the icon or the picture which represents it (or **Edit - Presentation Object - Show**).*

18

G-Transferring a presentation to another computer

This feature allows you to read a presentation on a computer which does not necessarily have PowerPoint installed.

Compressing a presentation onto floppy disks

- **File - Pack and Go**
- Click **Next**.
- Choose the presentation to compress then click **Next**.
- Choose the destination of the presentation (drive A if you are transferring to a floppy disk) then click **Next**.
- Activate the **Include Linked Files** option to include any linked files (sound, video, presentations ...) with the presentation.
- Activate **Embed True Type Fonts** to ensure that the fonts you have used are reproduced correctly then click **Next**.
- If PowerPoint is not installed on the destination computer, choose to have the PowerPoint viewer included in the package then click **Next**.
- Insert a blank, formatted disk into drive A then click **Finish**.
- ⇨ *You may need several floppy disks.*

Running a compressed presentation

The computer on which you wish to run the presentation must have Windows.

- The computer from which you are going to run the presentation must be equipped with Windows 95, 98 or NT.
- Decompress the presentation by running the **Pngsetup.exe** file from the floppy disk. Specify the destination folder.

The extraction can take several minutes.

- When the presentation has been completely decompressed, choose to view it.
- Open the folder where the decompressed files are located and double-click the file **Ppview.exe**: this starts the PowerPoint viewer.
- Double-click the name of the presentation that you want to see.
- At the end of the slide show, click the **End Show** button.

H-Exporting a presentation to Microsoft Word

The resulting Word document contains miniatures of the slides and the notes associated with them.

- **File - Send To - Microsoft Word**
- Choose the page layout that you want to apply to the Word document.
- Indicate whether the slides are to be embedded (**Paste**) or linked (**Paste link**) into the Word document.
- Click **OK** to start Word and create the new document.

⇨ *The command **File - Send To - Mail Recipient** exports the presentation as a message to a user of Outlook.*

3.2 Templates

A-Applying a design template to a presentation

A design template contains elements of formatting which can be applied all at once to define the overall look of a presentation.

▓ **Format**　　　　　　　　　　double-click the current template's
　Apply Design Template　　name (status bar)

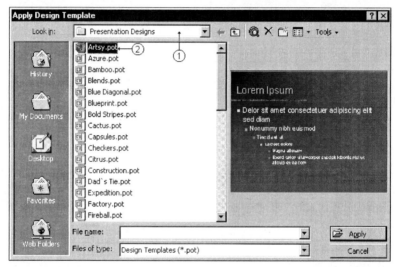

① Select the folder where the template you want is stored.

② Double-click the name of the template to apply it to the presentation.

⇨ *Templates have the extension POT.*

⇨ *The **Common Tasks** button on the **Formatting** toolbar contains the option **Apply Design Template**.*

B-Creating a design template

▦ In the slide master of an existing presentation, create the design that you want to save as a template.

▦ **File - Save As**

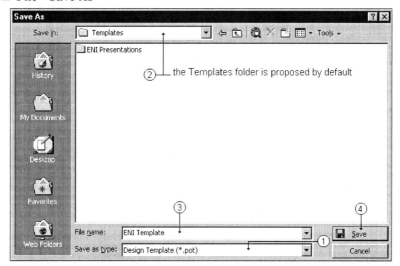

① Indicate that what you are creating is a template.

② Select the folder where you want to store it.

③ Give a name for the new template.

④ Save the template.

⇨ *The templates saved in the templates folder can be found under the* ***General*** *tab of the New dialog box.*

4.1 Slide shows

A-Running a slide show

▦ Activate the first slide that you want to see in the slide show.

▦ **View - Slide Show**
or
Slide Show - View Show

▦ If you have not set timings for the slide show, use the following methods of moving from slide to slide:

	🖰	🎲
Next slide	click with the left mouse button	Pg Dn , → , ↓ or the letter **N**
Previous slide		Pg Up , ← , ← , ↑ or the letter **P**
First slide		Home
Last slide		End

▦ If the slide show contains animations that have not been automated, use the space key to run each animation.

⇨ *To interrupt the slide show, press* Esc .

⇨ *To move to a specific slide, type its number then press* Enter .

⇨ *When you do not know a slide's number, you can reach it by choosing its title from a list: click with the RIGHT mouse button and take the options Go - By Title.*

B-Running a slide show continuously

▦ **Slide Show - Set Up Show**

▦ To run the slide show in a loop with five minutes between each show, choose **Browsed at a kiosk (full screen)**. When you activate this option, the **Loop continuously until "Esc"** option is activated automatically. You could also select this option alone.

C-Scrolling slides automatically in a slide show

▦ In Slide Sorter view select a slide, or a group of slides which you are going to display for the same length of time.

▦ **Slide Show**
Slide Transition

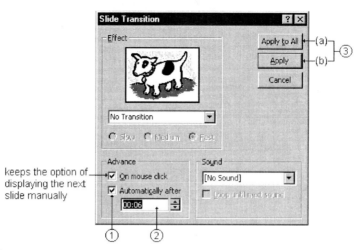

keeps the option of displaying the next slide manually

① Activate this option.

② Enter the length of time the slide(s) should stay on the screen.

③ Apply the new settings to all the slides (a), or just the slides you have selected (b).

⇨ *In Slide Sorter view, you can see the length of time during which each slide appears on the screen.*

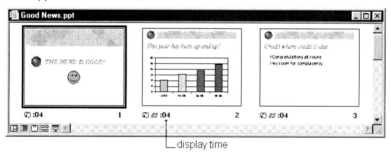

└─ display time

D-Adjusting the timing of a slide show

▓ Slide Show
Rehearse Timings

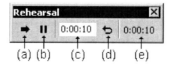

(a) (b)   (c)   (d)   (e)

▓ Click:

(a)	when enough time has passed.
(b)	to pause the timer (click it agin to restart).
(c)	to display the time for the active slide (can also be used to enter a precise time as hh:mm:ss).
(d)	reset the timer to zero
(e)	the total duration of the slide show.

▓ At the end of the rehearsal, click **Yes** to confirm the new slide timings.

▓ Click **No** in the new dialog box which appears: the Slide Sorter view is displayed more quickly.

E- Selecting the slides to include in the slide show

▓ **Slide Show - Set Up Show** or hold down the ⌈⇧ Shift⌉ key as you click ▣.

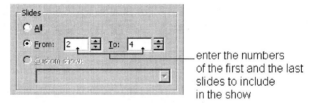

enter the numbers
of the first and the last
slides to include
in the show

⇨ *Activate the **All** option in **Slide Show - Set Up Show** to include all the slides again.*

⇨ *The ▣ tool allows you to start the slide show from the current slide.*

F- Working on slides during a slide show

Hiding a slide temporarily

▓ If you want the screen to go white, press the **W** or comma key. If you want the screen to go black press the **B** key or the semi-colon.

▓ Use the same key to display the slide again.

Writing on a slide

▓ Let the presentation run until it reaches the slide you want to write on. If the slide involves animations, wait until all the items you need on the screen are displayed.

▓ Press ⌈Ctrl⌉ **P**.

▓ Drag to draw or write on the slide. Keep the ⌈⇧ Shift⌉ key pressed down for perfectly straight horizontal or vertical lines.

▓ To erase the marks, type **E** on the keyboard. To erase the marks and go on with the slide show, press **N**.

To restore the pointer to its usual shape without losing the marks you have made on the slide, click with the right mouse button and choose **Pointer Options - Arrow**.

⇨ *The marks you make on the slide disappear once the slide show is over.*

⇨ *To change the colour of the pen, choose a new colour from the **Pen color** list in **Slide Show - Set Up Show**.*

G-Creating different slide shows for one presentation

Creating custom slide shows

Slide Show - Custom Shows

For each slide show, click the New button:

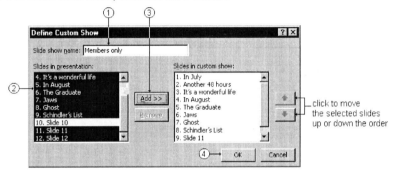

click to move the selected slides up or down the order

① Give a name for the slide show.

② Select the slides to include in the show (hold down ⇧ Shift or Ctrl as you click to select them).

③ Insert the slides.

④ Create the custom show.

Running a custom slide show

Slide Show - Custom Shows

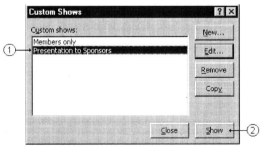

① Select the name of the show to run.

② Click to run the show.

Microsoft PowerPoint 2000

SLIDE SHOWS

H-Using the Meeting Minder

During a presentation, especially if it provokes a discussion among the participants, it is useful to be able to record observations and take notes on the spot.

During the slide show, press ⬚Shift ⬚F10 to display the slide show's shortcut menu and take the **Meeting Minder** option.

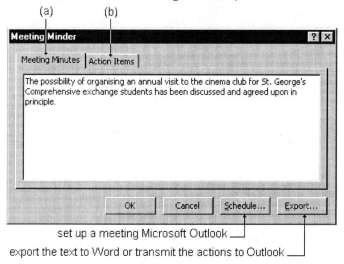

(a)   for noting down points to be remembered about the discussion. This can help with writing up the minutes, for example.

(b)   for making a list of things to be done after the slide show. These items are automatically displayed on a new slide, which appears at the end of the show.

⇨ *If the slide show is not running, you can consult the minutes and the list of actions via **Tools - Meeting Minder**.*

4.2 Special effects

A-Applying a transition effect to slides

A transition is the way in which a slide appears on screen during a slide show.

In Slide Sorter view, select the slides concerned by the same transition.

Slide Show
Slide Transition

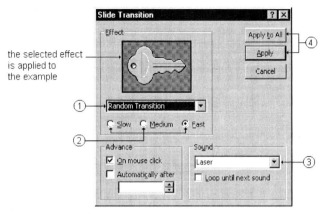

the selected effect is applied to the example

① Choose the transition effect.

② Choose the speed of the effect.

③ Associate a sound if you want to.

④ If only the selected slides are concerned, click **Apply**; if all the slides are concerned, click **Apply to All**.

▷ *You can select a transition effect in Slide Sorter view:*

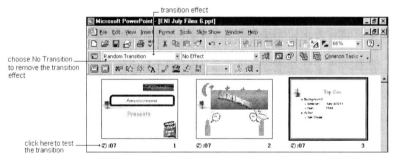

transition effect

choose No Transition to remove the transition effect

click here to test the transition

▷ *To interrupt the playing of a sound during a transition, go to the **Transitions** dialog box and choose **Stop Previous Sound** in the **Sound** list.*

B-Applying preset animation effects

▨ Display the **Animation Effects** toolbar by clicking [icon] (or **View - Toolbars - Animation Effects**).

Titles and body text

▨ Activate the slide you want to animate.

▨ Click one of these buttons from the **Animation Effects** toolbar:

  the title appears to fall in from above the slide.

  the body text appears in stages.

SLIDE SHOWS

Any slide object, including titles and body text

▓ Click the object to animate then click one of these buttons from the **Animation Effects** toolbar:

 The object "drives" in from the right accompanied by the noise of a car.

The object flies in from the left with a whooshing sound.

 The object appears as though seen through a camera shutter accompanied by the sound of a photograph being taken.

You see a flash of the object.

▓ The following animations can be applied to any item of text:

 The text flies in letter by letter from the top right of the window.

The text appears letter by letter accompanied by the noise of a typewriter.

 The text appears from the bottom up. This option is not available for titles.

The text appears to drop in, word by word, from above the screen.

⇨ *As soon as an object has been given an animation, its order number appear in the* Animation Order *list on the* Animation Effects *toolbar.*

C-Creating a custom animation effect

▓ Select the object concerned, click ▣ on the **Animation Effects** toolbar then activate the **Effects** tab.

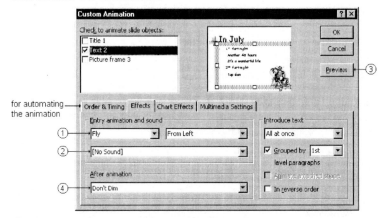

① Select the effect you want to apply.

② Select a sound to accompany the animation, if appropriate.

③ Check the result.

④ Indicate what should happen to the object once the animation is over.

⇨ *To remove an animation effect, select the item concerned and use **Slide Show - Preset Animation - Off**.*

⇨ *You can also apply an animation effect in Slide Sorter view:*

applies an animation effect to the slide's body text ⎯

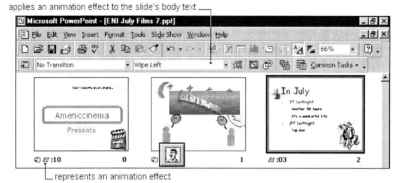

⎿ represents an animation effect

⇨ *During a slide show, the custom animation effect will not run unless you have previously set the slide show timings. If you have not done so, press* ⎡space⎤ *to see the object's animation. You can, of course, automate animation effects.*

D-Automating an animation

You can set animations to run automatically, so that you do not have to intervene during the slide show.

▓ Select the object associated with the animation, click [icon] on the **Animation Effects** toolbar then activate the **Order and Timing** tab.

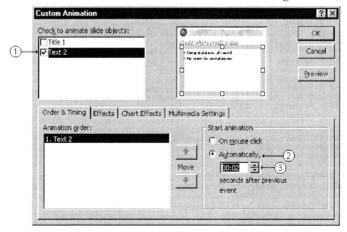

① Select the object concerned.

② Activate this option.

③ Indicate the time delay before the animation is to start.

E-Animating charts

▒ Select the chart you want to animate.

▒ Click the button on the **Animation Effects** toolbar and activate the **Chart Effects** tab.

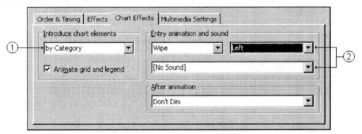

① Indicate the order in which the chart items should appear.

② Choose the animation effect and/or a sound to accompany the appearance of the chart.

F-Changing the order of a slide's animations

Changing the order of any object

▒ Click on the **Animation Effects** toolbar and activate the **Order and Timing** tab.

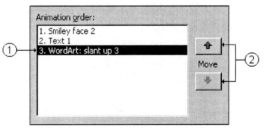

① Select the object.

② Move it up or down the order.

⇨ *To change the order of the selected effect, you can also select an order number on the Animation Effects toolbar.*

Changing the order in which text objects appear

Select the text concerned then click [icon] and activate the **Effects** tab.

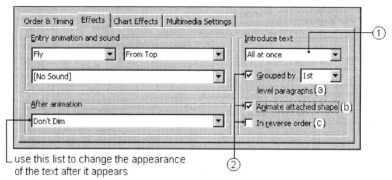

└ use this list to change the appearance
of the text after it appears

① Choose how to bring the text onto the slide.

② Use the following options to modify the effect:

(a)   the text appears one group of paragraphs at a time (how the paragraphs are grouped depends on the level selected in the list box).

(b)   if the text is in an AutoShape, activating this option will animate the text and the shape as one object. Leaving this option inactive will animate the text only.

(c)   the text appears starting with the last lines of the selected paragraph level.

5.1 Managing slides

A-Creating a slide

▒ Go to the slide after which the new one will appear.

▒ **Insert**   Ctrl **M**
  New Slide

▒ Choose the slide's layout then click **OK**.

⇨ *To create a new slide at the beginning of a presentation, activate Slide Sorter view and click in front of slide number 1.*

⇨ *When the insertion point is positioned in the text of a slide, you can create a new slide (with the same layout as the active slide) by pressing* Ctrl Enter *(this does not apply to a title slide).*

⇨ *To delete a slide in Slide Sorter view, select it and press* Del *. In slide view, use* **Edit - Delete Slide** *.*

B-Going to slides

▒ Use the following keys:

Pg Up / Pg Dn   previous/next slide.

Ctrl Pg Up or Home / Ctrl Pg Dn or End   first/last slide.

▒ In the slide pane view, use the ▲ and ▼ buttons or drag the cursor up or down the vertical scroll bar.

C-Selecting several slides

▒ Activate Slide Sorter view (▦).

▒ To select adjacent slides, click the first slide, hold the ⇧ Shift key down, and click the last slide.

▒ To select non-adjacent slides, click the first slide you want to select, hold down the Ctrl key, and click each of the slides you want to select.

▒ If you want to select all the slides, use **Edit - Select All** or Ctrl **A**.

⇨ *To deselect a slide, hold the* Ctrl *key down and click the slide.*

D-Copying/moving a slide

▧ In Slide Sorter view, select the slide to copy or move.

▧ If you want to move the slide, drag it to its new position. If you want to duplicate it, keep the `Ctrl` key pressed down as you drag the slide to its new position.

A vertical grey bar appears whenever you reach a position in between two existing slides.

▧ When the grey bar is at the position where you want to put the slide, release first the key, if you have been using it, then the mouse button.

⇨ *You can also use Copy/Cut - Paste or the Clipboard toolbar.*

E-Inserting slides from another presentation

▧ Display the slide before the position where you want to insert the new slides.

▧ **Insert - Slides from Files**

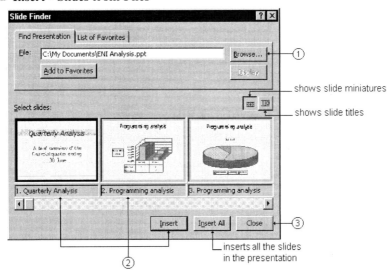

① Choose the presentation containing the slides to insert.

② `⇧ Shift`-click or `Ctrl`-click the slides that interest you to select them, then click **Insert**.

③ Close the dialog box.

⇨ *The slides are added to the active presentation. They adopt the attributes of the current template.*

F-Changing the layout of a slide

▓ Activate the slide concerned.

▓ Format - Slide Layout

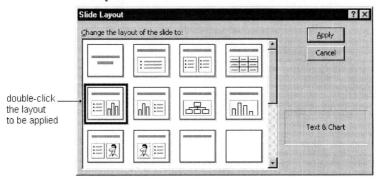

⇨ *The* **Common Tasks** *button allows you to access the* **Slide Layout** *option.*

G-Applying a customised background

▓ If you do not want to modify the backgrounds of all the slides, select the slides concerned, otherwise, display any slide.

▓ Format - Background

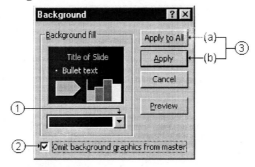

① Click here to fill the background with a **Color**, **Gradient**, a **Texture**, **Pattern** or a **Picture**.

② Activate this option to hide the background items defined in the master.

③ Apply the new background to all the slides (a) or just to the selected slides (b).

H-Customising slides using the masters

▦ For all slides except those with a **Title Slide** layout, go into the Slide Master to define the items which the slides have in common. To access the master, use:

View - Master - Slide Master or hold down ⌨ Shift while you click the 🔲 icon.

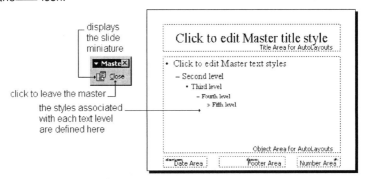

▦ For slides with a **Title Slide** layout, add the common items to the Title Master: **View - Master - Title Master**. If the active slide is a title slide, you can access the Title Master by holding down the ⌨ Shift key while you click the 🔲 button. If the command is unavailable, display the Slide Master then click 🔳.

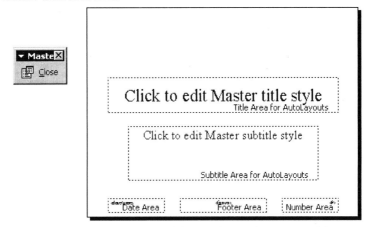

▦ Make the changes that you need to make to the master (changes you make to the master take effect in all the slides).

⇨ *To customise the presentation of slides when they are printed, work in the **Handout Master**.*

I- Numbering slides

▨ Depending on the slides you want to number, display:

The Slide Master	to number all the slides except for title slides.
The Title Master	to number the title slides.
A slide	to number either just the active slide or all the slides.

▨ Use the command **View - Header and Footer**

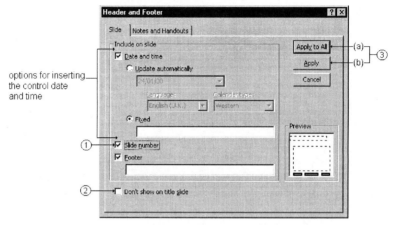

options for inserting the control date and time

① Activate this option.

② Do you want to number the title slide?

③ Number all the slides and their master (a) or number the active slide only (b).

▨ To change the position and format of slide numbers go into the Title Master or Slide Master and modify the **Number Area** (the # symbols).

⇨ *To number a particular set of slides, select them in Slide Sorter view. Use the **Apply** button to validate the command and close the **Header and Footer** dialog box.*

⇨ *Use **File - Page Setup - Number slides From** to define the number of the first slide in the presentation.*

J- Making a summary slide

▨ In **Slide Sorter** view, select the slides to be included in the summary.

▨ Click ▥ on the **Slide Sorter** toolbar.

K-Inserting comments into a slide

▨ Display the slide concerned in **Slide** or **Normal** view.

▨ **Insert - Comment** or ▨ on the **Reviewing** toolbar

▨ Type the comment and confirm by pressing ⌷Esc⌷.

▨ To hide the comment, or to display it when it is hidden use **View - Comments** or click ▨.

5.2 Colours

A-Applying a colour scheme

▨ Select the slide(s) concerned, or activate any slide.

▨ **Format - Slide Color Scheme**

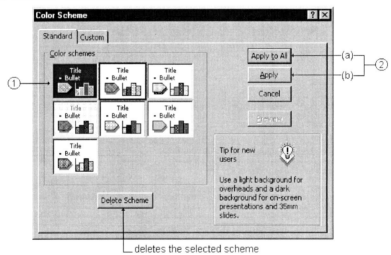

⌐ deletes the selected scheme

① Select the colour scheme you prefer.

② Apply the new colour scheme to all the slides in the presentation, and to the slide master (a) or just to the selected slides (b).

B-Copying the colour scheme of a slide

▨ Activate Slide Sorter view (⊞).

▨ Select the slide with the colour scheme you want to copy.

▨ To copy the scheme onto just one other slide, click the 🖌 button; to apply the scheme to more than one slide, double-click the 🖌 button.

▨ Click the slide(s) to which you want to apply the scheme.

▨ If you double-clicked the **Format Painter** tool, you will need to deactivate it when you have finished: click Esc.

C-Modifying a colour scheme

▨ Unless you want to change the colour scheme for all the slides, select the slide(s) concerned.

▨ **Format - Slide Color Scheme - Custom** tab

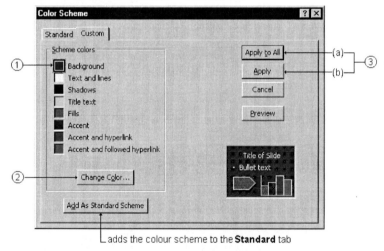

└ adds the colour scheme to the **Standard** tab

▨ For each slide item to which you want to apply a different colour:

① Select the item's current colour.

② Click this button and choose the new colour.

③ Apply the new colour scheme to all the slides in the presentation, and to the slide master (a) or just to the selected slides (b).

D-Creating a custom colour

▓ Open the colour dialog box of the item for which you want to create a new colour.

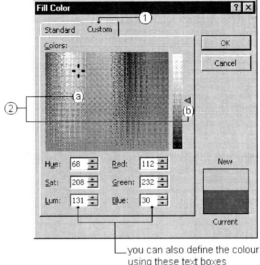

you can also define the colour using these text boxes

① Activate this tab.

② Customise the colour by dragging either the cross (a) or the arrow (b).

E-Displaying a presentation in black and white

▓ View
Black and White

▓ To customise the black and white scheme, right-click a space on the active slide then choose one of the options from the **Black and White** menu.

⇨ *To show colours again click the* *tool.*

6.1 Managing text

A-Entering text in a slide

Entering a title

▦ Click the placeholder which contains the text "Click to add title".

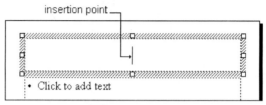

insertion point

• Click to add text

▦ Type in your title and click ⌨Esc to validate it.

Entering body text

▦ Select the space reserved for text, either by clicking the placeholder containing "Click here to add text" or by ⌨Ctrl ⌨Enter if the insertion point is in the title.

The text area becomes a frame with a hatched border and the insertion point appears, preceded by a bullet.

▦ Enter your text (PowerPoint takes care of the ends of lines) then use:

⌨Enter   to start a new paragraph
⌨⇧Shift ⌨Enter   to create a blank line with no bullet

▦ Give your paragraphs a level which reflects their importance: use ⌨⇄ (at the beginning of the line) or ⌨⇨ to demote a paragraph, ⌨⇧Shift ⌨⇄ or ⌨⇦ to promote a paragraph:

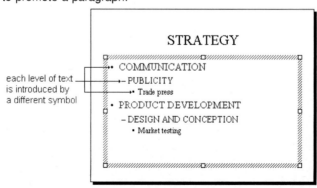

each level of text is introduced by a different symbol

STRATEGY

•• COMMUNICATION
  •– PUBLICITY
     •• Trade press
• PRODUCT DEVELOPMENT
  – DESIGN AND CONCEPTION
     • Market testing

⇨ *The style of each level is defined in the Slide Master.*

⇨ *All the text entered in the placeholders for title and body text appears in the Outline pane in the left of the window.*

⇨ *PowerPoint manages six outline levels: one level for the title and five levels for the text entered in the body text placeholder.*

⇨ *As you type, some words may appear underlined by a wavy red line. These are words that PowerPoint 2000 detects as misspelled.*

B-Using the Notes Page

▨ **View - Notes Page** or click in the Notes pane in Normal view.

▨ Go to the slide concerned and change the zoom if you need to.

▨ Click in the placeholder called **Click to add text** and type your notes.

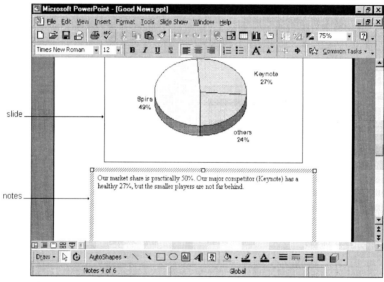

⇨ *To enter text in the notes pages during a slide show, right-click and choose* ***Speaker Notes.***

C-Modifying text

▨ Go the slide concerned and click the text object you want to modify.

▨ Make your changes. To add text, place the insertion point where it should appear and type.

▨ To delete the following character, press [Del]; to delete the previous character, use [←].

▨ To delete a group of characters, select and press [Del].

▨ Replace characters by selecting them and typing the new text.

D-Moving the insertion point inside a text object

▓ Use the following keys:

→/←	next/previous character
Ctrl → / Ctrl ←	beginning of next/previous word
Home / End	beginning/end of line
↓/↑	next/previous line
Ctrl ↓ / Ctrl ↑	beginning of next/previous paragraph
Ctrl Home / Ctrl End	beginning/end of text

E-Selecting text

▓ To select:

a word	double-click the word.
a paragraph	triple-click the paragraph.
a group of characters	either drag to select or click in front of the first character and hold down ⇧ Shift as you click just after the last character.

To select all the text in the text object, use **Edit - Select All** or Ctrl **A**.

⇨ *On the keyboard, hold down the* ⇧ Shift *key as you use the arrow keys to select.*

F-Copying/moving text

▓ Select the text or items concerned.

▓ To copy, use:

Edit **Copy**		Ctrl **C**
Edit **Cut**		Ctrl **X**

▓ Place the insertion point where you want to copy or move the item.

Edit **Paste**		Ctrl **V**

⇨ *If you can see the place where you want to insert the text, you can move a selection by dragging.*

⇨ *The Office Clipboard enables you to make multiple moves/copies.*

G-Correcting a misspelled word

When you make a spelling or typing error, PowerPoint detects it as soon as you have completed the word and typed a space or a punctuation mark after it. If PowerPoint can, it corrects the word automatically, otherwise it marks the word with a wavy red line. Right-click to correct it.

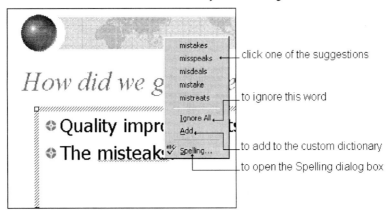

H-Checking your spelling

Position the insertion point at the top of the section that you want to check (to check the whole presentation, put it at the beginning).

Tools
Spelling

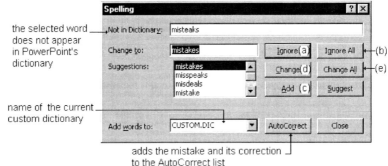

If it is a word which is correctly spelt but does not figure in the dictionary, click:

(a)   to leave the word as it is, and go on checking.

(b)   to ignore all occurrences of the word.

(c)   to add the word to the custom dictionary whose name appears in **Add words to** and go on checking.

If the word has been incorrectly spelt, click the correct version in the **Suggestions** list or type your own correction in the **Change to** box, then click:

(d)   to replace the selected word and continue checking.

(e)   to replace the word everywhere it occurs in the document.

⇨ *The options relating to the spelling check are available in* **Tools - Options, Spelling and Style** *page.*

⇨ *You can use the* **Tools - AutoCorrect** *command to create a list of your most frequent typing or spelling errors, so that Word can correct them automatically as you are typing.*

⇨ *To check a text written in a different language, use the command* **Tools - Language** *to set the language (preferably before you start typing the text).*

⇨ *When a light bulb appears in a slide, click it to open the style checker.*

I- Finding text

▓ Edit - Find or Ctrl F

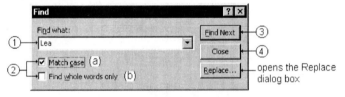

① Enter the text that you want to find.

② If necessary, activate the following options:

(a)   to find the word with the exact combination of upper and lower case letters that you have entered in the **Find what** box.

(b)   If the text you are looking for is a word and not a character string in any word.

③ Start searching; click again to find the next occurrence of the word.

④ Close the dialog box.

⇨ *Even after you have closed the* **Find** *dialog box, you can continue searching for the last word entered in* **Find what**, *by pressing* ⇧ Shift F4 .

J- Replacing text

▦ **Edit** - **Replace** or Ctrl **H**

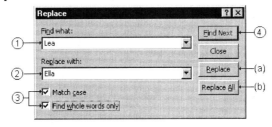

① Enter the text you want to find.

② Enter the text you want to replace it with.

③ Define your search and replacement criteria.

④ Start searching. Either make one replacement at a time (a) or choose to replace every occurrence without further confirmation (b).

6.2 Formatting characters

A- Changing the font/size of characters

▦ Select the text object or the characters concerned. To change the font used for all the paragraphs of a particular level, open the Slide Master and click the level concerned.

▦ Choose the font and the size from the lists on the **Formatting** toolbar.

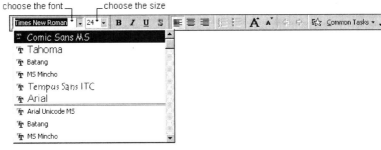

⇨ *You can also use the* ***Format*** *-* ***Font*** *command.*

⇨ *The* 🅰️ *tool applies the size just above the current size:* 🅰️ *applies the size just below it.*

B-Replacing a font

▨ **Format - Replace Fonts**

only the fonts used in the current presentation are listed

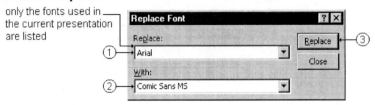

① Choose the font to replace.

② Chose the new font.

③ Make the replacement.

C-Applying attributes to characters

▨ Select the text object or the characters concerned. To set an attribute for all the paragraphs of a particular level, open the Slide Master and click the level concerned.

⌐🖰 ▨ Use the tool buttons to activate or deactivate the corresponding font styles:

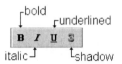

⬡ ▨ Use the appropriate shortcut keys:

Bold	Ctrl	**B**
Italic	Ctrl	**I**
Underlined	Ctrl	**U**

⇨ *You could also use the* **Format - Font** *command. The dialog box which opens also contains options for putting characters into superscript or subscript.*

⇨ *To remove all the attributes, use* Ctrl ⇧Shift *Z or* Ctrl space .

⇨ *To create a deeper shadow, first apply the* **Shadow** *attribute then click the* ▣ *button on the Drawing toolbar (after having activated the* **Shadow** *format).*

D-Changing the case of the characters

▨ Select the characters concerned.

▨ **Format - Change Case**

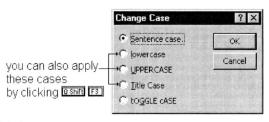

you can also apply these cases by clicking `⇑ Shift` `F3`

▓ Double-click the case you want.

E- Changing the text colour

▓ Select the text object or characters concerned. If this change concerns all the paragraphs of the same level, go to the slide master and click the corresponding paragraph.

▓ Open the 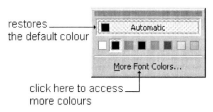 list on the **Drawing** toolbar and choose one of the basic colours:

restores the default colour

click here to access more colours

⇨ *You can also change the colour of a text by the **Format - Font** command.*

⇨ *Once you have applied a colour, it is shown on the* [A ▾] *tool. To apply the colour, click the tool.*

F- Copying text attributes

▓ Select the text whose attributes you want to copy.

▓ To copy the attributes just once, click the [🖌] button. To reproduce the same format several times, double-click the same button.

The mouse pointer takes the shape of a paint brush.

▓ Select the text to be formatted.

▓ If you double-clicked the **Format Painter** tool, you will need to deactivate it when you have finished: press `Esc`.

⇨ *The same tool can also be used to copy the attributes of an object.*

TEXT

6.3 Formatting paragraphs

A-Modifying the alignment of text

▦ Select a paragraph or a group of paragraphs that you want to align in the same way. To change the alignment of all the paragraphs of a particular level, open the Slide Master and click the level concerned.

▦ Use the **Format - Alignment** command or the following shortcuts:

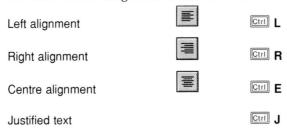

Left alignment   Ctrl L

Right alignment   Ctrl R

Centre alignment   Ctrl E

Justified text   Ctrl J

B-Spacing paragraphs

▦ Select the text object or the characters concerned. To create space around every paragraph of a particular level, open the Slide Master and click the level concerned.

▦ **Format - Line Spacing**

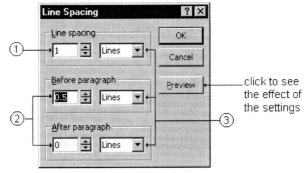

click to see the effect of the settings

① Indicate how much space to leave between the lines of the paragraph.

② Indicate how much space to leave before and/or after the paragraph.

③ Choose the unit of measurement.

⇨ *You can also use the* ⊟ *button to increase the spacing by 0.1 of a line, or the* ⊟ *button to decrease the spacing by 0.1 of a line.*

C-Changing the bullets

▨ Select the paragraphs or click in the paragraph concerned. If this change is to be applied to all the paragraphs of the same level, go to Slide Master and click the corresponding paragraph.

▨ **Formats - Bullets and Numbering - Bulleted** tab

▨ Click the **Character** button.

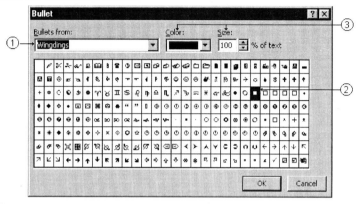

① Select the font.

② Click the symbol you want to zoom in on it.

③ Define the colour and size of the bullet.

▷ *To show or hide bullets in the selected text, click* ⊞.

D-Indenting paragraphs

To indent a line of text is to set it further from the margin. An indent can be applied to the first line only, or to all the text.

▨ Display the ruler (**View - Ruler**).

▨ Click inside the text object concerned. To set indents for all the paragraphs of a particular level, open the Slide Master and click the level concerned.

▨ Drag the indent markers along the ruler to set the indents:

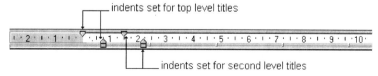

indents set for top level titles

indents set for second level titles

▽ first line indent

△ hanging indent (all lines except the first)

▫ left indent of the whole paragraph

E-Managing tabs

Setting tab stops

▦ Display the ruler (**View - Ruler**).

▦ Click inside the text object concerned (the tab stops will be applied to all the paragraphs in the object).

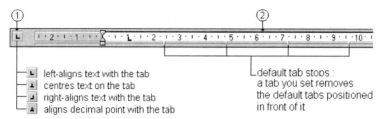

① Click here as many times as is necessary to select the type of tab.

② Click the position where you want to put the new tab.

Using tab stops

▦ Press ⬚ or, if you're at the beginning of a line, press Ctrl Alt ⬚ to move the text on to the next tab stop. Press ⬚ to move it back to the one before.

⇨ *To move a tab stop, drag it along the ruler. Drag the tab stop off the ruler to remove it.*

6.4 Outline view

A-Creating slides and adding text in Outline view

▦ Enter the title of the new slide then press Ctrl Enter to start typing the bulleted text (or press Enter to go from the title directly into a new slide).

▦ Type the bulleted text as if you were in Slide view.

▦ When you have finished the bulleted text, press Ctrl Enter to create a new slide.

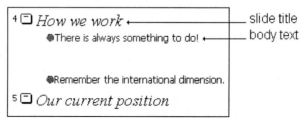

⇨ *You can also work in the Outline pane in Normal view.*

B-Changing the display in Outline view

▨ Show the **Outlining** toolbar if necessary (**View - Toolbars - Outlining**).

▨ Use the [A/A] button on the **Outlining** toolbar to hide the formatting and to make it visible again.

▨ To display just the titles, click [icon].

▨ To display all the text, including titles, click [icon].

▨ To view the text linked to the title currently containing the insertion point, click [icon].

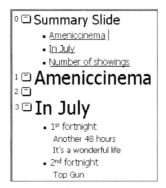

▨ To hide the text linked to the title where the insertion point is positioned, click [icon].

⇨ *You can also work in the Outline pane in Normal view.*

C-Moving paragraphs in Outline view

▨ Place the insertion point in the paragraph to move. If this is a title with lower-level text attached to it, collapse the title.

▨ Point to the bullet in front of the paragraph to move.

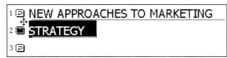

▨ Drag the line to its new position.

⇨ *When you want to move a title just one place up or down the order, click inside it and use* [icon] *or* [icon].

D-Inserting an Outline file into a presentation

▨ Activate the slide before the position where you are going to insert the new slides, created from the data in the outline.

Insert - Slides from Outline

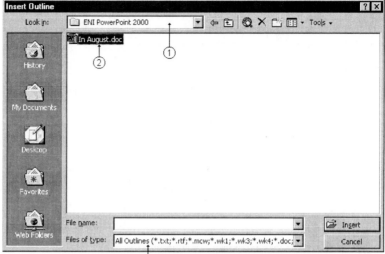

⌐ the file type All Outlines is selected automatically

① Open the folder which contains the document.

② Double-click the name of the document you want to insert.

⇨ *PowerPoint creates a new slide for every top-level title ("Heading 1") in the outline: the top-level heading becomes the slide title. The other heading levels become levels of bulleted text.*

E-Saving an outline file

By saving the outline as a file, you can use it for more than just the presentation.

▦ **File - Save As**

▦ Give a file name then select the drive and the folder.

▦ In the **Save as type** list, choose **Outline/RTF**.

⇨ *The document created can be exploited not only in PowerPoint but also in other applications such as Microsoft Word. In PowerPoint, the name of the outline file does not appear on the title bar.*

F-Opening an outline file

You can create a new presentation simply by opening an outline file.

▦ **File**   [icon]   Ctrl O
Open

▦ Open the **Files of type** list and choose **All Outlines**.

▦ Double-click the name of the outline file.

7.1 Drawing

A-Drawing a common shape

▦ Display the slide concerned in Slide or Normal view.

▦ On the **Drawing** toolbar, click [line icon] to draw a line, [arrow icon] for an arrow, [rectangle icon] for a rectangle, or [oval icon] for an oval, then drag to draw.

▦ To draw one of the AutoShapes, open the **AutoShapes** list on the **Drawing** toolbar.

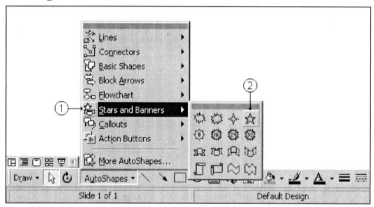

① Point to the category which interests you.

② Select the shape that you want to draw.

▦ Drag to draw the AutoShape.

⇨ *If you want the drawing tool to remain active, so that you can draw several similar objects, double-click it. When you have drawn all the objects, press* Esc .

⇨ *To draw a regular shape (one which fits perfectly inside a square) hold the* ⇧ Shift *key down as you drag to draw the shape.*

⇨ *To draw a shape around its central point, hold down the* Ctrl *key as you drag to draw.*

B-Linking two shapes with a connector line

A connector line is a line between two objects which continues to link them even if they change position.

▦ Open the **AutoShapes** list, select the **Connectors** category and choose the most suitable style of connector line.

▦ Start from a connection site on the first object and drag across to a connection site on the second object.

OBJECTS

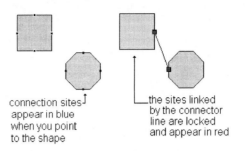

connection sites
appear in blue
when you point
to the shape

the sites linked
by the connector
line are locked
and appear in red

▧ To move a connector line, drag either end of the line to a different connection site.

▧ To detach a connector line, drag from the middle of the line (the connectors appear in green).

C-Replacing one shape by another

▧ Select the shape to replace.

▧ Open the **Draw** list and click **Change AutoShape**.

▧ Select the category then the new shape.

D-Creating a text box

▧ In Slide or Normal view, use **Insert - Text Box** or click the 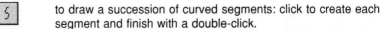 tool.

▧ Drag the mouse to draw the text box.

▧ Type the text.

⇨ *To present text in a non-rectangular shape, replace the text box with a different shape or create a new shape and type your text.*

E-Drawing freehand

▧ Display the slide concerned in Slide or Normal view.

▧ Open the **AutoShapes** list and point to **Lines**.

▧ Click the button that corresponds to what you want to draw:

⟋	to draw a succession of curved segments: click to create each segment and finish with a double-click.
⟍	to draw a freeform, including both curved and straight segments: click to create straight segments, drag to create curved ones and finish with a double-click.
✎	to draw as if you were drawing with a pencil (PowerPoint calls this type of drawing a scribble): release the mouse button to finish.

F-Modifying a freehand drawing

▨ Select the drawing to modify.

▨ In the **Draw** list on the Drawing toolbar, click the **Edit Points** option.

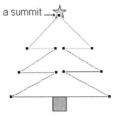

a summit

▨ Drag a summit to move it.

▨ To delete a summit, hold down [Ctrl] [⇧ Shift] as you click it.

▨ To add a summit, hold down [Ctrl] as you click the line.

G-Adjusting an object's shape

Objects such as arcs, crosses or triangles can be adjusted in this way.

▨ Select the object:

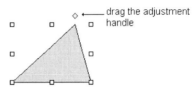

drag the adjustment handle

H-Changing a line into an arrow

▨ Activate the slide concerned in Slide or Normal view.

▨ Draw the line that is to become an arrow. This line must not be a closed shape.

▨ Click the **Arrow Style** [⇄] tool on the **Drawing** toolbar.

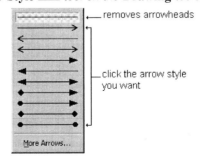

removes arrowheads

click the arrow style you want

7.2 Pictures

A-Inserting a Clip Art picture

In order to use all the pictures on the CD-ROM, you need to install the Clip Gallery on your disk. Insert the CD-ROM into the drive and leave it there.

▓ **Insert**
Picture
Clip Art

▓ If necessary, activate the **Pictures** tab and select a category.

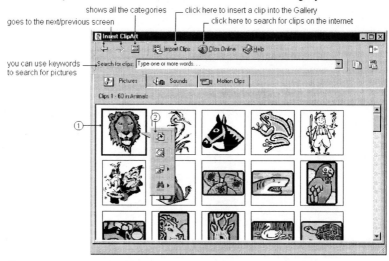

shows all the categories — click here to insert a clip into the Gallery
goes to the next/previous screen — click here to search for clips on the internet
you can use keywords — to search for pictures

① Select the required picture.

② To insert the picture, click the [icon] icon on the toolbar that appears.

⇨ *To import a picture from a file, use **Insert - Picture - From File**.*

⇨ *To insert a picture, you can also reduce the window by clicking [icon],
and drag the picture to the slide.*

⇨ *To frame a picture, select it then use the [icon] tool on the **Picture** toolbar.*

B-Changing the colours in a picture

▦ Select the picture concerned and click the ▣ button on the **Picture** toolbar.

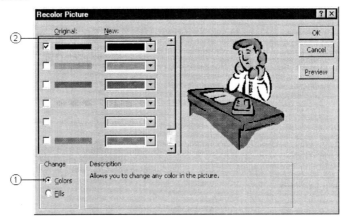

① Check that this option is active.

② For each colour that needs replacing, open the list and choose the new colour.

C-Managing colour, brightness and contrast

▦ Select the picture concerned then click ▣ on the **Picture** toolbar.

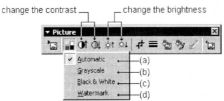

▦ Choose the appropriate option:

(a) to use the picture's colours normally.

(b) to transform a coloured picture into a black and white picture, replacing the colours with shades of grey.

(c) to transform a coloured picture into a black and white one which does not include any grey.

(d) to increase the brightness and diminish the contrast, making the picture ideal for use as a watermark.

⇨ *You could also use the options in **Format - Picture**, on the **Picture** tab.*

⇨ *To restore the original picture select the picture then click* ▣ *on the* ***Picture*** *toolbar.*

OBJECTS

D-Managing Clip Art categories

▦ To create a new category, click the **New Category** button, name the category, and click **OK**.

▦ To rename or delete a category, right-click it and choose either **Rename Category** or **Delete Category** (when you delete a category, the clips it contains are not deleted).

E-Adding a picture to the Clip Gallery

▦ Click the **Import Clips** button.

▦ Go to the folder that contains the picture you want to add and double-click the pictures name.

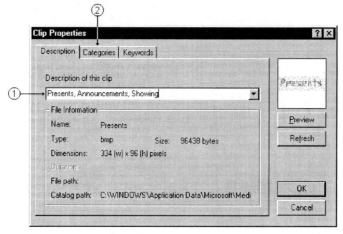

① Type the keywords to be associated with the picture.

② Click this tab to select the categories the picture is to be inserted into.

F-Cropping a picture

▦ Select the picture concerned and click the button on the **Picture** toolbar.

╪ ←drag one of the sizing handles to focus on a detail

7.3 Importing objects

A-Inserting a sound object

A sound from the gallery

In order to be able to use all the sounds available on the CD-ROM, you need to install the Clip Gallery on your computer.

▓ If necessary, insert the CD-ROM in the drive.

▓ Activate the slide concerned.

▓ **Insert**
Movies and Sounds
Sound from Gallery

▓ Select a category.

▓ Click the sound you want then click the [icon] icon to insert the sound into the slide.

▓ Indicate whether the sound is to be played automatically during a slide show.

Another sound

▓ Activate the slide concerned.

▓ **Insert - Movies and Sounds - Sound from File**

▓ Go to the folder that contains the sound and double-click its name.

▓ Indicate whether the sound is to be played automatically during a slide show.

A sound object is shown as a speaker:

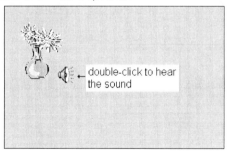

B-Preventing a sound or movie from interrupting the slide show

By default, a slide show stops when a slide containing a sound or movie appears.

Select the object in question.

Click 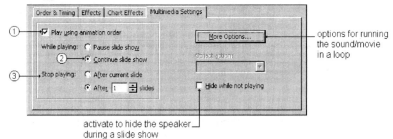 on the **Animation Effects** toolbar and choose the **Multimedia Settings** tab.

① options for running the sound/movie in a loop

activate to hide the speaker during a slide show

① Select this option.

② Activate this option.

③ Indicate when the sound or movie is to stop playing. If the clip is to play throughout the slide show, enter the total number of slides in the show.

⇨ *This action is also possible for an OLE object.*

⇨ *You can also find the **Loop until stopped** option, which allows you to repeat a sound, in the **Edit - Sound Object** dialog box.*

⇨ *To interrupt the sound while an object animation plays, go to its animation effects, activate the **Effects** tab and select **No Sound** in the second list in the **Entry animation and sound**.*

C-Inserting a motion clip from the Office 2000 CD-ROM

To make use of all the clips on the CD-ROM, you need to install the Clip Gallery on your computer.

Insert the CD-ROM in the drive.

**Insert
Picture
Clip Art**

Activate the **Motion Clips** tab and select a category.

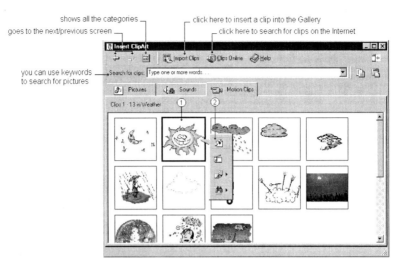

shows all the categories ⎯⎯⎯⎯⎯⎯⎯⎯
goes to the next/previous screen ⎯⎯⎯

click here to insert a clip into the Gallery
click here to search for clips on the Internet

you can use keywords ⎯⎯⎯ to search for pictures

① Select the motion clip you want.

② Click the [▣] tool to insert the clip into the side.

⇨ *The motion clip will run automatically during a slide show.*

⇨ *You can also use* **Insert - Movies and Sounds - Movie from Gallery.**

D-Inserting any external object

There are two ways of inserting an object from another application: ***lin-king*** *and* ***embedding****. An embedded object has no existence outside the document where you have inserted it. The only way to edit an embedded object is to open the presentation containing it. If, on the other hand, you link an object into a presentation, you establish a connection between the PowerPoint document and the original document in the server application. You can edit the original document independently of the presentation then decide whether or not to update the presentation.*

▓ **Insert - Object**

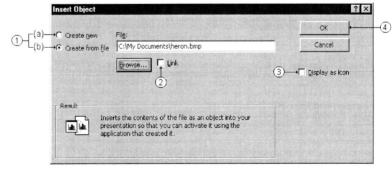

OBJECTS

① If the object does not exist yet, choose (a) then indicate what type of object it is that you are going to create. If the object already exists, choose (b) then use the **Browse** button to select the corresponding document.

② Activate this option if you prefer to establish a link with the server application, rather than embedding the object.

③ Activate this option if you want the object to be represented in the presentation by an icon.

④ Insert the object.

▨ If necessary, create the object in its server application (which opens automatically) then click the slide to restore PowerPoint's toolbars and menus.

▨ To edit the object (whether it is embedded or linked into the presentation), double-click it to start the server application.

▨ If you are working with a linked object, use the command **Edit - Links** to manage the link between the presentation and the document in the server application:

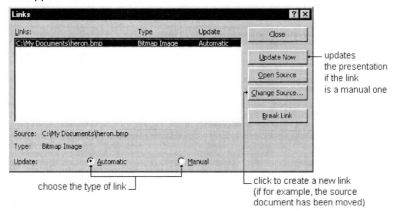

⇨ *To create an Excel object, select **Microsoft Excel Worksheet** in the Object type list. Enter your data then reduce the object's frame so that only the cells containing data are shown.*

E- Inserting a WordArt object

WordArt applies special typographic effects to a text.

▨ **Insert**
   Picture
   WordArt

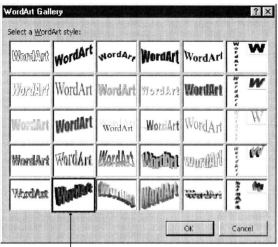

— double-click the effect to apply

Enter the text to which you want to apply the effect. If necessary, format it.

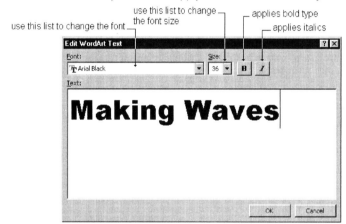

Click **OK** to insert the WordArt text, and, if necessary, move the object to a different position on the slide.

⇨ *To edit a WordArt object, double-click it.*

OBJECTS

7.4 Organisation charts

A-Inserting an organisation chart

▨ In a slide with a **Organization Chart** layout, double-click the placeholder. In any other slide, use **Insert - Object - MS Organization Chart 2.0**.

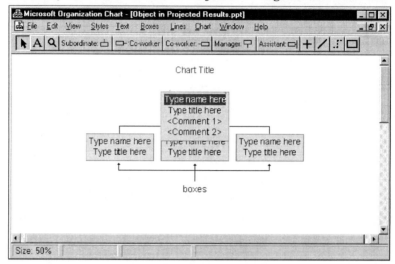

Microsoft Organisation Chart is a server application.

▨ Once you have created the organisation chart, leave the application by closing its window. The chart which appears in the presentation is an embedded object. If you need to edit the chart, double-click it: this starts the application **Microsoft Organization Chart 2.0**.

⇨ *Use **Chart - Background Color** to change the organisation chart's background colour.*

⇨ *To modify the default organisation chart, use the command **Edit - Options**.*

⇨ *To change the zoom, use the **View** menu.*

B-Managing boxes in an organisation chart

Filling in a box

▨ Click the box to select it.
▨ Enter the text, using [Enter] to move down to the next line.

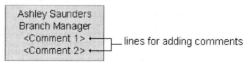

Adding/deleting a box

▨ To add a box:

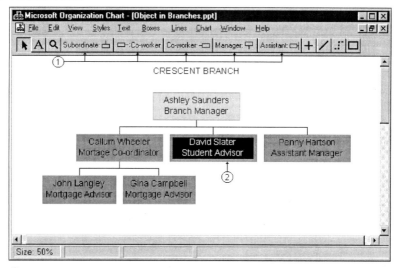

① Click the button corresponding to the type of box to add.

② Click the box to which you want to link the new box then fill in the new box.

▨ To delete a box, select it then press ⌊Del⌋ (or **Edit - Clear**).

⇨ *When you have selected a box, you can add boxes using the following keys:* ⌊F2⌋ *for a subordinate,* ⌊F3⌋ *for a colleague on the left,* ⌊F4⌋ *for a colleague on the right,* ⌊F5⌋ *for a manager and* ⌊F6⌋ *for an assistant.*

⇨ *You can create up to 50 subordinate levels.*

C-Selecting differents items

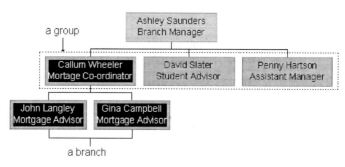

OBJECTS

To select	Method
a box or several boxes	click the first and ⎇Shift-click the others
all the boxes	Ctrl A
a group	Ctrl G
a branch	Ctrl B

⇨ *You can select any of the elements mentioned above with the command* **Edit - Select**. *To select by level use* **Edit - Select Level**.

D-Changing the appearance of boxes

▨ To change the style of a group, select the group concerned and choose one of the options from the **Styles** menu.

▨ To change the look of boxes, select the box(es) to modify and set the options available through the **Boxes** menu.

⇨ *The* **Lines** *menu contains options for changing the look of the lines linking the boxes.*

E-Managing text

▨ To insert unattached text, click the ⎀A tool, click the place where you want to insert the text, type the text, and then press ⎋Esc when you have finished.

▨ Use the **Text** menu to format selected text.

▨ To add a title to the organisation chart, select the **Chart Title** text and type the title.

⇨ *If you do not enter a title, PowerPoint uses the slide title.*

F-Making a drawing

▨ Display the drawing tools:

View - Show Draw Tools or Ctrl **D**

▨ Click the button which corresponds to what you want to draw:

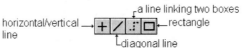

horizontal/vertical line — diagonal line — a line linking two boxes — rectangle

▨ Drag to draw.

7.5 Tables

A-Creating a table

▓ Activate the slide in which you want to insert a table.

▓ **Insert - Table** (or double-click the placeholder in the slide).

▓ Indicate the number of rows and columns you want to create in the dialog box and confirm with **OK**.

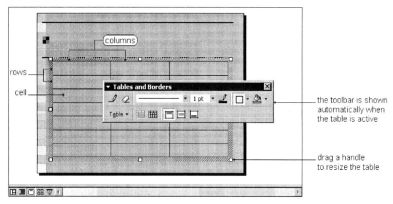

⇨ *A table can have up to 25 rows and 25 columns.*

⇨ *The* ▦ *tool on the **Standard** toolbar allows you to create a table.*

⇨ *You can also use the* 🖊 *tool on the **Tables and Borders** toolbar to draw a table. Drag to draw the outline of the table then draw the rows and columns in the same way.*

⇨ *To move a table, point to the edge of the table and wait for a four-headed arrow to appear. Drag the table to move it.*

B-Entering data in a table

▓ Activate the cell in which you want to enter data by clicking or using the keys:

⇄/⇧Shift ⇄   Cell to the right/left.

↑/↓   Cell above/below.

▓ Enter the cell contents then activate the next cell.

⇨ *The* Enter *key allows you to insert a paragraph break inside a cell.*

C-Selecting cells

▨ To select:

A cell   drag over the cell or use ⇄ and ⇧ Shift ⇄.

A column place the pointer above the column and, when the pointer becomes a black arrow, click.

A row   activate a cell in the row in question, click the Table ▾ button on the **Tables and Borders** toolbar and click **Select Row**.

The table activate a cell in the table, click the Table ▾ button and choose **Select Table**.

▷ *You can also select several cells by dragging.*

D-Merging cells

▨ Select the cells you want to merge.

▨ Click the ⊡ button on the **Tables and Borders** toolbar.

▷ *The ⬦ tool on the Tables and Borders toolbar can also be used. Drag over the dividing line you want to remove.*

▷ *To split the selected cells, use the ▦ tool or click the ∥ tool and draw the dividing line.*

E-Formatting text in cells

▨ Select the cell(s) concerned.

▨ Use the tools on the **Formatting** toolbar as you would for the body text of a slide.

▨ To change the vertical alignment of the cells, click on the alignment you want on the **Tables and Borders** toolbar:

🔲   Aligns the text at the top of the cell.

🔲   Aligns the text in the centre of the cell.

🔲   Aligns the text at the bottom of the cell.

▷ *To insert a tab stop in a cell, do as you would in a slide.*

F-Changing the appearance of cells

▨ Select the cell(s) concerned, or the entire table.

▨ To apply a colour and/or pattern to cells, open the list on the 🎨 ▾ tool and select a colour or pattern.

- To change the cell borders, open the list on the [tool image] tool then choose the style you want.

- Open the list on the [1 pt] tool to choose a different line weight.

- Use the [tool image] tool to choose a colour for the border.

- To change the type of border, open the list on the [tool image] tool.

⇨ *You can also use Format - Tables - Borders tab, or the Borders and Fill option in the* [Table ▾] *list.*

⇨ *To remove a border, click the* [Table ▾] *button, choose the Borders and Fill option and click the border you want to remove on the example shown in the dialog box.*

G-Managing rows and columns

Inserting a row or column

- Select a cell in the row or column after which you want to insert the new row or column.

- Click the [Table ▾] button on the **Tables and Borders** toolbar and choose the appropriate option depending on where you want to insert the row/column.

Deleting a row or column

- Click in a cell in the row or column you want to delete.

- Click the [Table ▾] button and choose **Delete Columns** or **Delete Rows**.

Changing the width of a column/height of a row

- Point to the vertical line to the right of the column or the horizontal line underneath the row.

  The mouse pointer becomes a double-headed black arrow.

- Drag the mouse pointer to achieve the required width or height.

⇨ *To adjust the width of a column to fit its contents, double-click the vertical line to the right of the column.*

H-Copying Excel data into PowerPoint

- Copy the Excel data to the clipboard.
- Place the insertion point where the data are to appear.
- To paste without linking, use:

Edit
Paste

 V

OBJECTS

▓ To paste the data as a hyperlink, use **Edit - Paste as Hyperlink**.

The data appear as a hyperlink (underlined text). Click the link during a slide show to open the source Excel data.

▓ To paste the data and establish a link at the same time, use **Edit - Paste Special**, and activate the **Paste link** option. In the **As** list, select the object type and click **OK**.

All modifications made to the Excel data will be updated in PowerPoint.

7.6 Managing objects

A-Selecting objects

▓ To select an item of text point to the frame surrounding the text: when the pointer takes the shape of four arrows, click.

▓ To select any other object, click it.

▓ To select several objects at once [⇧ Shift]-click them or activate the tool and drag to enclose the objects to select.

▓ To select all the objects, use **Edit - Select All** or [Ctrl] **A**.

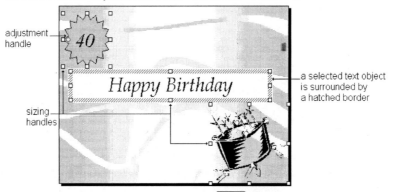

adjustment handle

sizing handles

a selected text object is surrounded by a hatched border

▓ To deselect one of the selected objects, [⇧ Shift]-click it again.

⇨ *In Slide Sorter view, you can select a set of slides.*

B-Deleting objects

▓ Select the object(s) then press [Del].

⇨ *You can also use **Edit - Clear**.*

C-Copying/moving an object

From one slide to another

- Select the object(s) to copy or move.
- To copy the object:

Edit Ctrl **C**
Copy

- To move the object:

Edit Ctrl **X**
Cut

- Activate the slide where you want to put the objects.
- To paste the object:

Edit Ctrl **V**
Paste

⇨ *The Clipboard toolbar appears automatically when you make the second consecutive copy (see Making multiple copies/moves).*

Inside a slide

- Select the object(s) to copy or move.
- Drag the object to its new position. To copy, hold down the Ctrl key as you drag the object to the place where you want to copy it.

⇨ *If you hold the Shift key down as you drag, the object can only move horizontally or vertically.*

⇨ *If the Snap - To Grid option from the Draw list on the Drawing toolbar is active, the object is attracted to the nearest point on an invisible grid. To position an object freely when the grid is active, hold down the Alt key while you are dragging.*

⇨ *In Slide Sorter view, you can use these techniques to copy and move slides.*

Duplicating an object

- Select the object(s) that you want to duplicate.
- **Edit - Duplicate** or Ctrl **D**
- Reposition the duplicate, if necessary.

effect obtained after ⟶
eight duplications

D-Making multiple copies/moves

If necessary, display the **Clipboard** toolbar.

This toolbar opens automatically when you make a second consecutive copy.

Each selection is added to the clipboard and is represented by an icon.

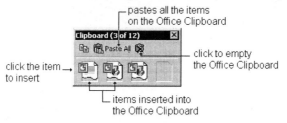

⇨ *The Office Clipboard can hold up to 12 items. When you try to copy any more items, a message appears asking if you want to delete the first item copied to the clipboard.*

⇨ *Once the **Clipboard** toolbar has been activated, it appears in all the Microsoft Office applications.*

E-Copying object attributes

Select the object whose attributes you want to copy.

If you only want to make one copy, click the [icon] tool. Double-click the same tool to make several copies.

The mouse pointer becomes a paintbrush.

Select the object you want to format.

Leave the process by pressing Esc.

⇨ *You can also use this action to copy the attributes of text.*

F-Aligning objects on a grid

Open the **Draw** list on the **Drawing** toolbar and point to the **Snap** option.

Activate:

To Grid   so that the object will be aligned on an invisible grid when you move it by dragging.

To Shape   so that the object is aligned along the edges of other shapes when you move it by dragging.

G-Positioning an object precisely

▦ Select the object concerned.

▦ **Format - Colors and Lines - Position** tab

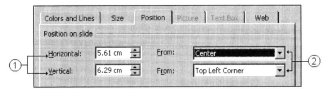

① Indicate the space to leave between the left edge/top of the object and the part of the slide defined in **From**.

② Do you want to position the object in relation to the top left corner or centre of the slide?

H-Aligning objects

▦ Select the objects concerned.

▦ Open the **Draw** list on the Drawing toolbar and choose the **Align or Distribute** option.

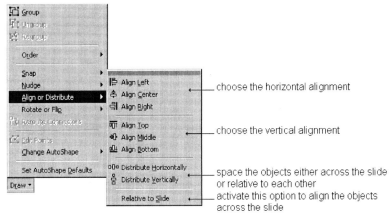

choose the horizontal alignment

choose the vertical alignment

space the objects either across the slide or relative to each other

activate this option to align the objects across the slide

I- Resizing an object

▦ Select the object concerned.

▦ **Format - Colors and Lines** - **Size** tab

OBJECTS

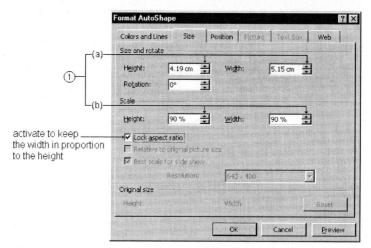

① Enter the object's new dimensions either in centimetres (a) or as a percentage (b).

Select the object:

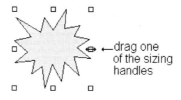

drag one of the sizing handles

➪ If you hold the ⌘Ctrl key down as you drag, the object is resized in all directions from its central point.

➪ If you drag one of the handles at a corner of the selection frame, the proportions of the object are conserved.

J- Changing an object's orientation

Select the object concerned.

Open the **Draw** list on the **Drawing** toolbar and select the **Rotate or Flip** option.

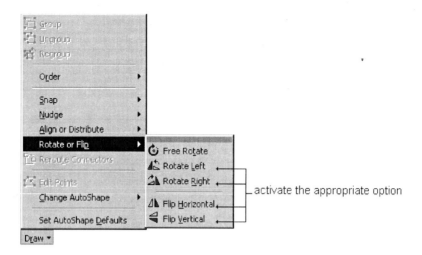

activate the appropriate option

K-Changing the order in which objects overlap

▦ Select the object that needs to come forward or to go further back.

▦ Open the **Draw** list on the Drawing toolbar and select the **Order** option.

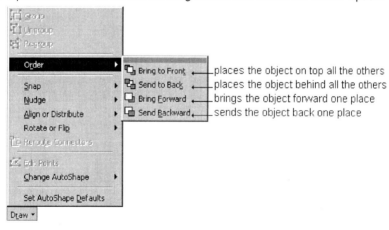

places the object on top all the others
places the object behind all the others
brings the object forward one place
sends the object back one place

L- Grouping/ungrouping objects

Grouped objects behave as if they were a single object: you can move them, resize them and so on all at once.

▦ Select the objects to group, or the group that you are going to split up.

▦ Open the **Draw** list on the Drawing toolbar.

▦ Activate the **Group** option or the **Ungroup** option.

⇨ *The **Draw - Regroup** command groups the ungrouped objects.*

OBJECTS

M-Associating an action with an object

▥ Select the object then use **Slide Show - Action Settings**.

▥ If the action is to occur after a mouse-click, activate the **Mouse Click** tab. If the action is to happen when you point to the object, activate the **Mouse Over** tab.

▥ Select the action you want.

⇨ *If you insert an action button from the AutoShapes list on the Drawing toolbar, the Action Settings dialog box opens automatically.*

7.7 Formatting objects

A-Framing an object

▥ Click the object in question.

▥ **Format - Colors and Lines**

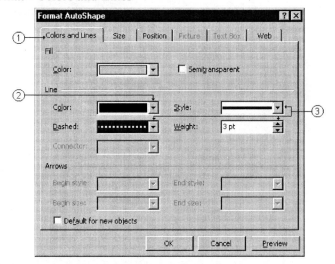

① If necessary, activate this tab.

② Select the colour of the frame.

③ Define the appearance of the lines in the frame.

⇨ *The* 🖋 *tool on the Drawing toolbar gives access to most of the options proposed in Format - Colors and Lines.*

⇨ *To remove a frame, open the* 🖋 *list and choose No Line.*

B-Positioning text inside an object

▨ Click in the text you want to position.

▨ **Format - Colors and Lines - Text Box** tab

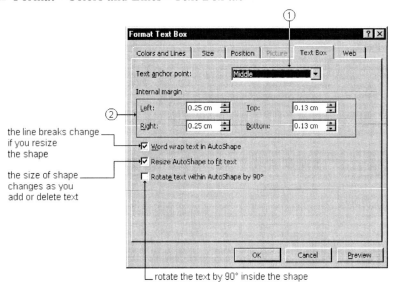

the line breaks change
if you resize
the shape

the size of shape
changes as you
add or delete text

rotate the text by 90° inside the shape

① Select the text alignment.

② Indicate the margins to be applied between the edges of the object and the text.

C-Free-rotating an object

▨ Select the object then click [⟳] on the **Drawing** toolbar.

▨ Drag one of the green circles.

▨ Leave the process by clicking [⟳] again, or by pressing [Esc].

⇨ *You can also enter a **Rotation** value under the Size tab, **Format - Colors and Lines**.*

OBJECTS

D-Applying a fill colour to an object

▨ Select the object then click the 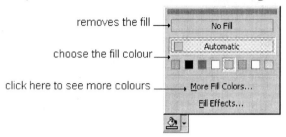 tool on the **Drawing** toolbar.

removes the fill →

choose the fill colour →

click here to see more colours →

⇨ *To dim the fill colour, activate the Semitransparent option in the Format - Colors and Lines dialog box.*

E-Filling an object with a gradient

▨ Select the object and click the 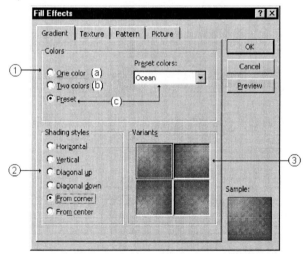 tool then choose **Fill Effects** (**Gradient** tab).

① Choose a colour scheme: one colour (a), two colours (b) or a preset scheme (c).

② Choose the style of gradient.

③ Choose a variant.

F- Filling an object with a pattern

▓ Select the object and click the [icon] tool then **Fill Effects**.

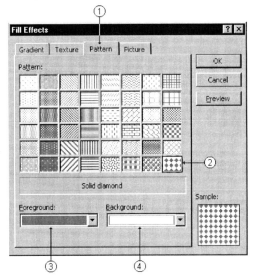

① Click this tab.

② Choose a pattern.

③ Choose the foreground colour.

④ Choose the background colour.

⇨ *The **Texture** and **Picture** tabs in the **Fill Effects** dialog box allow you to insert a texture or a picture as the object fill.*

G-Applying a 3-D effect

▓ Select the object and click [icon] on the **Drawing** toolbar.

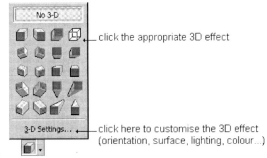

click the appropriate 3D effect

click here to customise the 3D effect (orientation, surface, lighting, colour...)

⇨ *The [icon] tool allows you to apply a shadow to an object.*

OBJECTS

Microsoft PowerPoint 2000

H-Changing the appearance of lines

 Select the lines in question.

 Click one of the following buttons and choose an option:

   to change the colour of the lines.

   to change the weight of the lines.

   to change the style of the lines.

⇨ *These tools can also be used to define the border of an object or the frame of a picture.*

⇨ *To remove a line or a frame, open the*   *list and choose* **No Line**.

8.1 Creating/editing a chart

A-Inserting a chart into a slide

▨ Display the slide where you want to insert the chart.

▨ In a slide with a **Chart** layout, double-click the placeholder, or in any other slide, use **Insert - Chart** or ▨.

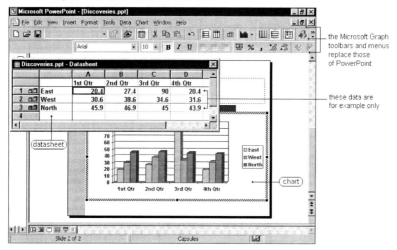

the Microsoft Graph toolbars and menus replace those of PowerPoint

these data are for example only

▨ To leave Microsoft Graph 2000, click the slide outside the chart object.

▨ To edit a chart on a slide, double-click the chart.

CHARTS

B-Changing the chart type

░ **Chart - Chart type**

activate to restore the default chart

hold down this button to see a preview

① Select the basic type of chart.

② Select one of the variants proposed.

⇨ *You can also choose a basic chart type from the* 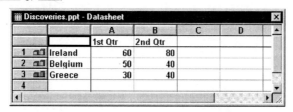 *list.*

⇨ *You can change the type for a single series: select the series before you use the command.*

C-Deciding whether series represent rows or columns

░ Choose the appropriate option from the **Data** menu or use the buttons 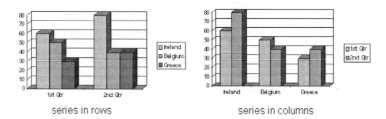 or [ ] .

series in rows   series in columns

D-Inserting the data table into a chart

Click the  tool to insert into the chart a table showing the data from the datasheet. The same tool button removes a data table from a chart.

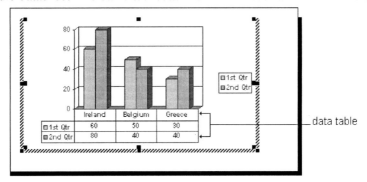

data table

⇨ *You can also use **Chart - Chart Options - Data Table** tab, and activate the **Show data table** option.*

E-Changing the appearance of the data table

Click the chart to activate it.

Point to the data table and check that **Data Table** appears in a Screen-Tip before you click to select it.

Format
Selected Data Table   Ctrl 1

text formatting options

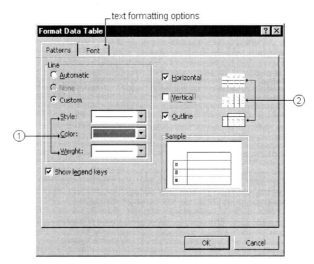

① Customise the table's border.

② Indicate the lines which should appear.

CHARTS

8.2 The data represented by the chart

A-Looking at the datasheet

▓ A datasheet is made up of 4000 rows and 4000 columns:

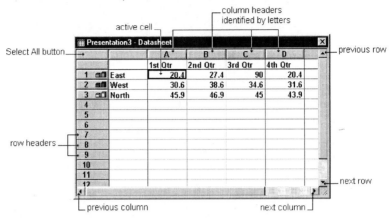

▓ To hide or display the datasheet, use:

View
Datasheet

▓ To move the pointer, use the following keys:

↑/↓	next/previous row
→ or ⇄	next column
← or ⇧ Shift ⇄	previous column
Pg Dn/Pg Up	the screen below/above
Home/End	the first column/the last column which contains data
Ctrl Home/Ctrl End	the first/last cell containing data

▓ To select a range of cells, drag over the cells or shift-click them (click the first cell and hold down ⇧ Shift as you click the last).

▓ To select a row or a column, click the row/column header or press ⇧ Shift space for a row and Ctrl space for a column.

▓ To select the entire datasheet, click the **Select All** button or press Ctrl **A**.

B-Entering data

▓ Activate the first cell you want to fill in.

▓ Type the data then go to the next cell and continue the data entry.

⇨ *To change a cell, double-click it or press* F2.

⇨ *You can also paste data that you have previously copied into the clipboard.*

C-Deleting data and/or formatting

▦ Select the cells containing the data to delete.

▦ **Edit - Clear**

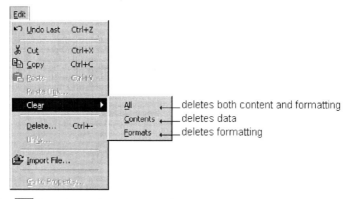

deletes both content and formatting
deletes data
deletes formatting

⇨ *The ⌷Del⌷ key clears the contents of the selected cells.*

D-Deleting rows or columns

▦ Select the rows or columns to delete.

▦ **Edit - Delete** or ⌷Ctrl⌷ **-** (minus sign)

⇨ *Delete with caution: Microsoft Graph does not ask for confirmation.*

E-Inserting rows or columns

▦ Select the row or the column which comes after the position where you want to insert the new one.

▦ **Insert - Cells** or ⌷Ctrl⌷ **+**

⇨ *To insert several rows or columns, select as many rows/columns as you want to insert.*

F-Changing the widths of columns

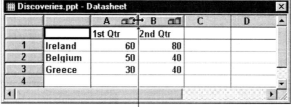

drag to the width you want or double-click
to fit the column to its contents

CHARTS

⇨ *You could also use **Format - Column Width**. In the dialog box which appears, there is an option which returns the column to the standard width.*

G-Changing the number format

▨ Select the cells concerned.

▨ Click the appropriate tool button to format numerical values:

  to present the number as a currency value.

  to present it as a percentage: this style multiplies numbers by 100.

  to separate thousands with a comma.

  to increase the number of decimal places.

  to decrease the number of decimal places.

▨ To format the data in the sheet, use the buttons on the toolbar or **Format - Font**.

⇨ *These formats concern the datasheet in its entirety.*

⇨ *If the format you need does not appear on the Formatting toolbar, use the command **Format - Number**.*

⇨ *The chart scale takes the format of the numerical data in the first series.*

H-Excluding data from the chart

▨ Select the row(s) or column(s) containing the data to exclude.

▨ **Data - Exclude Row/Column**

⇨ *The excluded data appears in grey in the datasheet.*

⇨ *To put excluded data back into the chart, select the row(s) or column(s) concerned and use **Data - Include Row/Column**.*

I- Importing Excel data in Microsoft Graph 2000

▨ **Edit**
Import File

▨ Select the name of the Excel workbook then the name of the worksheet that contains the data you want to import.

▨ Choose to import the **Entire sheet** or a **Range** of cells.

▨ If necessary, deactivate **Overwrite existing cells** then click **OK**.

8.3 Chart options

A-Selecting chart objects

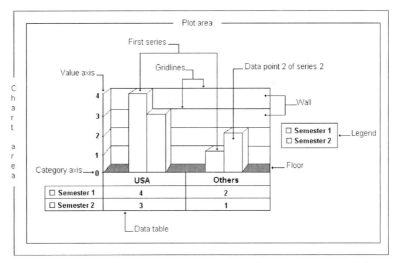

▨ To select a chart object, point to the object, check the name which appears in the ScreenTip and click, or open the **Chart Objects** list and click the name of the object to select.

Chart Objects list

▨ To select a data point in a series, click it once to select the series, then once more to select the point itself.

▨ The easiest way to select an axis is to click one of its data labels.

▨ To select a text object, click inside the text then press Esc.

⇨ *If no ScreenTip appears when you point to an object, open the **Tools - Options** dialog box at the **Chart** page and activate the **Show names** option under **Chart Tips**.*

CHARTS

B-Managing the legend

▧ To reposition the legend, drag it to its new location or use **Format - Selected Legend - Placement** tab.

▧ To hide the legend, select it and click ⌈Del⌋.

▧ To display the legend again, activate the **Show legend** option in **Chart - Chart Options - Legend** tab.

C-Managing axes

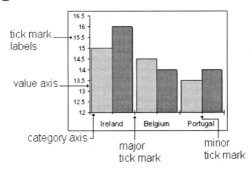

▧ To hide or display an axis, use **Chart - Chart Options - Axes** tab.

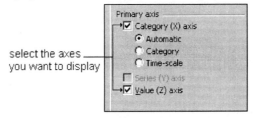

⇨ *If Microsoft Graph detects two chart types in the same chart, this dialog box contains two frames: the* **Primary Axis** *frame, which concerns the axis of the basic chart, and the* **Secondary Axis** *frame, which concerns a separate chart type applied to one or more series.*

- To change the look of an axis, double-click it to open the **Format Axis** dialog box (or use **Format - Selected Axis**):

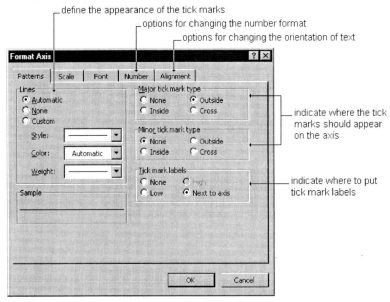

define the appearance of the tick marks

options for changing the number format

options for changing the orientation of text

indicate where the tick marks should appear on the axis

indicate where to put tick mark labels

- To change the scale, double-click the value axis:

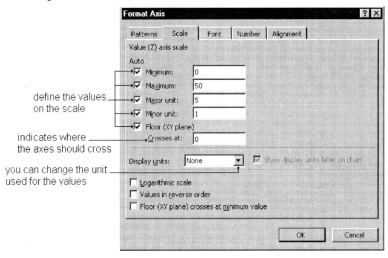

define the values on the scale

indicates where the axes should cross

you can change the unit used for the values

D-Managing text in a chart

▨ To add a title: **Chart - Chart Options - Titles** tab

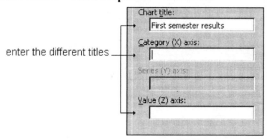

enter the different titles

▨ Click the title to change it (you can use the `Enter` key to add more lines).

▨ To enter unattached text, make sure that no text item is selected. Type the text then press `Esc` to confirm.

The inserted text is a text box. It is inserted in the middle of the chart, but you can move it.

▨ To format text in a chart, select the text item then use the buttons on the toolbar or use **Format - Font - Font** tab.

▨ To change the orientation of text in a chart, select the item and use **Format - Font - Alignment** tab.

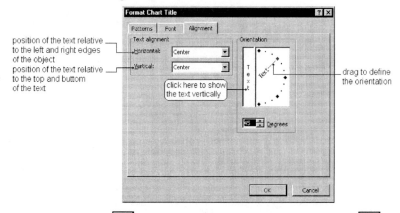

position of the text relative to the left and right edges of the object

position of the text relative to the top and buttom of the text

drag to define the orientation

⇨ *You can also use* ▨ *to rotate the text downwards by 45°, or* ▨ *to rotate the text upwards by 45°.*

E-Managing chart objects

▨ To move an object, select it and drag it to its new position.

▨ To resize the selected object, drag one of the selection handles.

Some objects (such as titles) cannot be resized.

▓ To frame and apply a fill to an object, select it and use **Format - Font - Patterns** tab.

choose a background colour

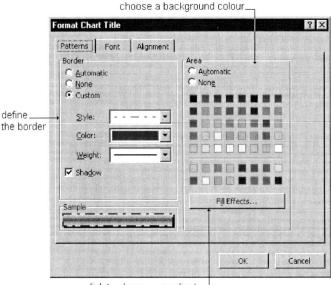

define the border

click to choose a gradient, texture, pattern or picture

⇨ *You can also use the* 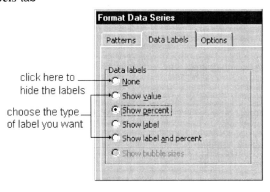 *list to colour an object.*

F-Showing data labels

▓ If the data label concerns only one point in a series, select this point. If the labels concern the whole series, select the series.

▓ **Format - Selected Data Series**
Data Labels tab

click here to hide the labels

choose the type of label you want

G-Adding gridlines to a chart

▓ **Chart - Chart Options - Gridlines** tab

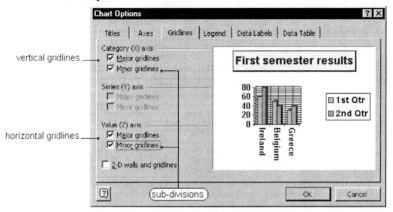

H-Overlapping columns/bars and spacing categories

Data markers can only overlap in a column chart or a bar chart.

▓ You could also double-click the column or bar and activate the **Options** tab.

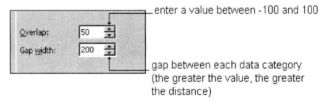

I- Restoring the default chart

A single command cancels all the changes you have made to a chart.

▓ Use the command **Chart - Chart type - Default formatting**.

⇨ *In Microsoft Graph 2000, **Edit - Undo** or* *or* Ctrl **Z** *only undoes the last action.*

J- Options available for line charts

▒ To display a trendline, use **Chart - Add Trendline**:

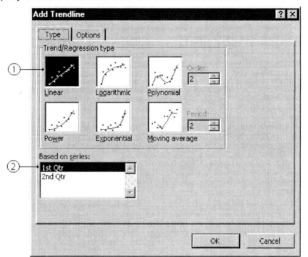

① Select the type of trend line to create.

② Choose the series concerned.

*To customise a trendline, select it and use **Format - Selected Trendline**.*

▒ To change the look of a line, double-click it (or use **Format - Selected Data Series - Patterns** tab).

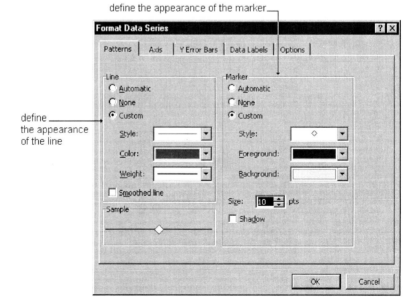

K-Changing a 3-D chart

▓ Chart - 3-D View

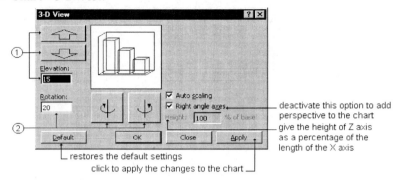

① Define the elevation.

② Rotate the plot area.

L- Options available for pie charts

▓ To explode a slice, select the slice in question and drag it out of the chart.

▓ To rotate the chart, select a slice and use **Format - Selected Data Point - Options** tab. In the **Angle of first slice** box, enter the degree of rotation you want.

9.1 Macros

A-Creating a macro

▓ **Tools - Macros - Record New Macro**

▓ Name the new macro.

▓ If there is more than one presentation open, select the one to which the macro is relevant in the **Store macro in** list.

▓ Fill out the information about the macro and click **OK**.

▓ Carry out all the actions that you want to include in the macro.

▓ Click ■ on the **Stop Recording** toolbar (or **Tools - Macro - Stop Recording**).

B-Running a macro

▓ **Tools - Macro - Macros** or ⟨Alt⟩ ⟨F8⟩

▓ If necessary, open the **Macro in** list to choose the presentation containing the macro.

▓ Double-click the macro to run.

➪ *The presentation that contains the macro you want must be open for you to see it in the **Macro in** list.*

➪ *To edit a macro, **Tools - Macro - Macros**, select the macro in question and click **Edit**.*

➪ *To delete a macro, **Tools - Macro - Macros**, select the macro in question and click **Delete**. Confirm by clicking **Yes**.*

10.1 Electronic Mail

A-Sending a slide as the message body

This feature means that the message recipient can see the contents of a slide even if PowerPoint is not installed on his/her computer.

▓ Open the presentation that contains the slide you want to send, or create it, and activate the slide in question.

▓ **File - Send To - Mail Recipient** or 🖾

▓ Leave the **Send current slide as message body** option, then click **OK**.

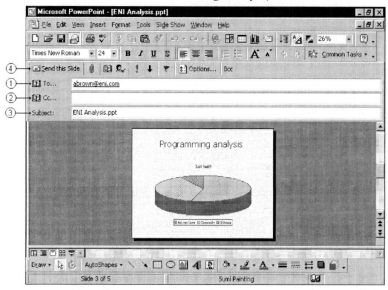

This screen may differ depending on the e-mail software you are using. The slide appears as the message body.

① Enter the address(es) of the recipient(s).

② Enter the address(es) of the recipient(s) of the copy of the message.

③ Give your message a subject.

④ Send the slide.

⇨ *To send a presentation as an attachment, use* ***File - Send To - Mail Recipient (as Attachment)***.

B-Broadcasting a presentation

When you broadcast a presentation, users will be able to see the presentation in the browser even if they do not have PowerPoint.

Scheduling a broadcast

▒ Open the presentation you want to broadcast.

▒ **Slide Show - Online Broadcast - Set Up and Schedule**

The first time you use this feature, a message may appear asking you to install the necessary application.

▒ Leave the **Set up and schedule a new broadcast** option and click **OK**.

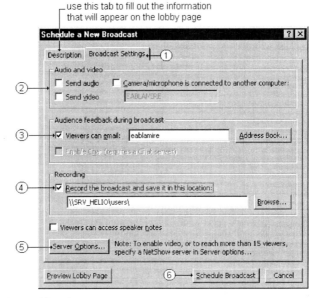

use this tab to fill out the information that will appear on the lobby page

① Activate this tab.

② Activate these options if you want to play sound or movie files during the slide show (if the presentation includes a video, you need to use Netshow).

③ Activate this option if you want to be able to receive comments during the presentation.

④ Do you want to save the broadcast in a shared folder so that the recipients can view it later?

⑤ Click here and fill use the text box in the **Step 1** frame to give the name of the shared folder on a file server which will contain the presentation during the broadcast. If you are broadcasting the presentation to more than 15 users, you will need to specify a NetShow server in **Step 2**.

⑥ Confirm by clicking here.

Microsoft PowerPoint 2000

- If you have chosen not to use a NetShow server a message appears to remind you that you cannot broadcast your presentation to more than 15 people. Answer **Yes** or **No**.
- Choose the recipients and the date and time of the broadcast.

  The contents of the lobby page are shown in the message body.
- Send the message by clicking **Send** and validate the confirmation message.

Starting the broadcast

- Open the presentation you want to broadcast.
- **Slide Show - Online Broadcast - Begin Broadcast**
- Test the microphone if necessary, then close the dialog box.

  PowerPoint counts down to the start time you set for the broadcast. When the counter reaches zero, a message appears prompting you to start the broadcast.

  If you want to start the broadcast before the prearranged time, use the Start *button.*
- Click **Yes** when the message to begin the broadcast appears.
- If necessary, scroll the slides.

⇨ *You can change the settings for the broadcast or the time at which it will take place via* **Slide Show - Online Broadcast - Set Up and Schedule***: take the* **Change settings or reschedule a broadcast** *option.*

Watching a presentation broadcast

- Activate your e-mail program and open the message inviting you to the broadcast.

  The message contains a hyperlink.
- Click it, activate the **Open it** option, and click **OK**.

  Your browser opens and displays the lobby page and the time remaining before the start of the broadcast.
- Once the broadcast is finished, you can close the browser.

⇨ *If you receive a reminder message, click the button* **Start Broadcast** *to start the broadcast.*

⇨ *The* **View Previous Slides** *button allows you to see all the slides during the broadcast.*

10.2 Searching the Web

A-Searching Internet sites

▧ Display the **Web** toolbar then click the ▧ tool.

The Microsoft home page appears in the browser window.

▧ Type the keywords of your search in the appropriate text boxes. Use the following techniques:

This search:	will find pages containing:
Toowoomba flower	either the word "Toowoomba" or the word "flower".
+Toowoomba+flower	both words
"Toowoomba flower"	the expression "Toowoomba flower"
+Toowoomba+flower-florist	the words "Toowoomba" and "flower" but not "florist"
flower*	the words "flower", "flowers" etc

▧ Confirm your search by pressing ⌨Enter. After looking at the results, close the browser window.

B-Looking for help on the Microsoft site

▧ **Help - Office on the Web**

▧ Carry out your search.

▧ When you have finished, close the browser window.

10.3 Web pages

A-Creating and looking at a Web page

You can publish information on your company's intranet and/or the Internet. The first step is to create a Web page.

▧ Open the presentation you want to use to create your Web page.

▧ **File - Save as Web Page**

▧ Indicate where you want to save the web page and its file name and click *Save*.

Web pages have the extension .html.

▧ To see a Web page, open the page you want to see then use **File - Web Page Preview**.

The Web page opens in the browser and is shown as it would appear on an intranet and/or the Internet. There are two panes. Use the pane on the left to select the slide you want to see.

▓ Close the browser once you have seen all the slides.

⇨ *Most Web pages are made up of the items (bullets, backgrounds, pictures, charts...), which are, by default, stored in a folder called a "supporting files folder". This folder is automatically created in the folder that contains the Web page. If you move, copy or delete the Web page, you must also move, copy or delete this folder.*

B-Publishing a Web page

Creating a Web folder

▓ **File**
   Open   Ctrl O

▓ Click the **Web Folders** button on the **Places** bar.

▓ Click the tool to create a new folder.

▓ Enter the URL address of your Web server in the appropriate text box and click **Next**.

▓ Enter the name of the folder in the **Enter the name for this Web Folder** box, then click **Finish**.

▓ Close the **Open** dialog box by clicking ☒.

Publishing a Web page

To do this you need to have created a Web folder (see the section above).

▓ Open the Web file (htm format).

▓ **File - Save as Web Page**

▓ Click the **Web Folders** shortcut then double-click the name of the folder in which you want to publish your Web page.

▓ If necessary, change the page's title (which will appear on the browser's title bar) using the **Change Title** button.

▓ Change the **File name**, if necessary, and click **Save**.

All Internet and/or intranet users can now admire your Web page.

Moving around in text

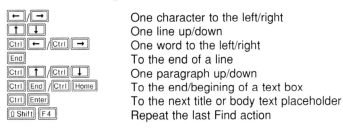

← / →	One character to the left/right
↑ ↓	One line up/down
Ctrl ← / Ctrl →	One word to the left/right
End	To the end of a line
Ctrl ↑ / Ctrl ↓	One paragraph up/down
Ctrl End / Ctrl Home	To the end/begining of a text box
Ctrl Enter	To the next title or body text placeholder
⇧ Shift F4	Repeat the last Find action

Deleting text

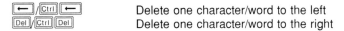

← / Ctrl ←	Delete one character/word to the left
Del / Ctrl Del	Delete one character/word to the right

Selecting text and objects

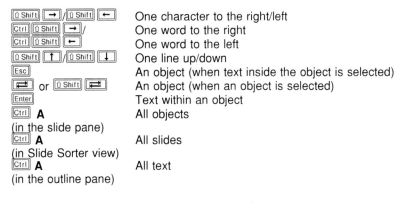

⇧ Shift → / ⇧ Shift ←	One character to the right/left
Ctrl ⇧ Shift → /	One word to the right
Ctrl ⇧ Shift ←	One word to the left
⇧ Shift ↑ / ⇧ Shift ↓	One line up/down
Esc	An object (when text inside the object is selected)
⇄ or ⇧ Shift ⇄	An object (when an object is selected)
Enter	Text within an object
Ctrl A	All objects
(in the slide pane)	
Ctrl A	All slides
(in Slide Sorter view)	
Ctrl A	All text
(in the outline pane)	

Slide show

N/ Enter / Pg Dn	Next animation or next slide
(or click the mouse)	
P/ Pg Up	Previous animation or slide
"number" + Enter	Go to slide "number"
B or full-stop	Display a black screen
W or comma	Display a white screen
S or plus sign (+)	Stop or restart an automatic slide show
Esc	End a slide show
E	Erase on-screen annotations
H	Go to next hidden slide
T	Set new timings
O	Use original timings
M	Use mouse-click to advance
Ctrl P	Change the pointer to a pen
Ctrl A	Change the pointer to an arrow
Ctrl H	Hide the pointer and button immediately

Microsoft PowerPoint 2000

Ctrl U		Hide the pointer and button in 15 seconds
⇧ Shift F10		Display the shortcut menu
⇄ / ⇧ Shift ⇄		Go to the next/previous hyperlink

Working in an outline

Alt ⇧ Shift ← /		Promote/demote a paragraph
Alt ⇧ Shift →		
Alt ⇧ Shift ↑ /		Move selected paragraphs up/down
Alt ⇧ Shift ↓		
Alt ⇧ Shift 1		Show heading level 1
Alt ⇧ Shift +		Expand text below heading
Alt ⇧ Shift -		Collapse text below heading
Alt ⇧ Shift A		Show all text or headings
slash (/) on the number pad		Turn character formatting on or off

Miscellaneous shortcut keys

⇧ Shift F10		Display a shortcut menu
Alt space		Display the application's **Control** menu

Menu shortcut keys

File

Ctrl N		New
Ctrl O		Open
Ctrl S		Save
Ctrl P		Print
Alt F4		Exit
Ctrl W		Close

Edit

Ctrl Z		Undo
Ctrl Y		Repeat
Ctrl X		Cut
Ctrl C		Copy
Ctrl V		Paste
Del		Clear
Ctrl ⇧ Shift C		Copy formats
Ctrl ⇧ Shift V		Paste formats
Ctrl A		Select all
Ctrl D		Duplicate
Ctrl F		Find
Ctrl H		Replace

View

`F5`   Run Slide Show

Insert

`Ctrl` **M**   New slide
`Ctrl` **K**   Hyperlink

Format

Font
`Ctrl` `⇧ Shift` **F**   Font
`Ctrl` **B**   Bold
`Ctrl` **I**   Italics
`Ctrl` **U**   Underline
`Ctrl` `⇧ Shift` **P**   Font Size
`Ctrl` **+**   Subscript
`Ctrl` `⇧ Shift` **=**   Superscript
`Ctrl` `space`   Remove formatting

Alignment

`Ctrl` **L**   Left
`Ctrl` **E**   Center
`Ctrl` **R**   Right
`Ctrl` **J**   Justify
`⇧ Shift` `F3`   Change the case

Tools

`F7`   Spelling
Macro
`Alt` `F8`   Macros
`Alt` `F11`   Visual Basic Editor

Window

`F6`   Next pane
`⇧ Shift` `F6`   Previous pane

Help

`F1`   Microsoft PowerPoint Help
`⇧ Shift` `F1`   What's This?

SHORTCUT KEYS

Standard toolbar

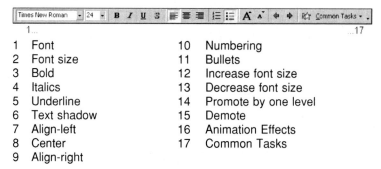

1	New	12	Repeat
2	Open	13	Hyperlink
3	Save	14	Tables and Borders
4	Electronic mail	15	Insert a table
5	Print	16	Insert a chart
6	Spelling	17	New slide
7	Cut	18	Expand all
8	Copy	19	Show formatting
9	Paste	20	Grayscale
10	Paste format	21	Zoom
11	Undo	22	Microsoft PowerPoint Help

Formatting toolbar

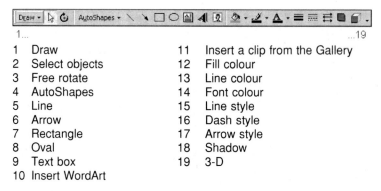

1	Font	10	Numbering
2	Font size	11	Bullets
3	Bold	12	Increase font size
4	Italics	13	Decrease font size
5	Underline	14	Promote by one level
6	Text shadow	15	Demote
7	Align-left	16	Animation Effects
8	Center	17	Common Tasks
9	Align-right		

Drawing toolbar

1	Draw	11	Insert a clip from the Gallery
2	Select objects	12	Fill colour
3	Free rotate	13	Line colour
4	AutoShapes	14	Font colour
5	Line	15	Line style
6	Arrow	16	Dash style
7	Rectangle	17	Arrow style
8	Oval	18	Shadow
9	Text box	19	3-D
10	Insert WordArt		

Slide Sorter toolbar

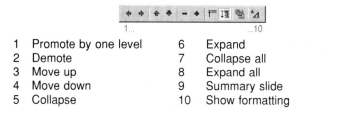

1...   ...9

1	Transition	6	Check timing
2	Transition effects	7	Summary slide
3	Animation effects	8	Speaker's notes
4	Animation preview	9	Common Tasks
5	Hide slide(s)		

Outlining toolbar

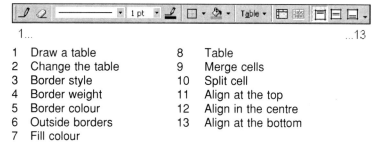

1...   ...10

1	Promote by one level	6	Expand
2	Demote	7	Collapse all
3	Move up	8	Expand all
4	Move down	9	Summary slide
5	Collapse	10	Show formatting

Tables and Borders toolbar

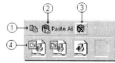

1...   ...13

1	Draw a table	8	Table
2	Change the table	9	Merge cells
3	Border style	10	Split cell
4	Border weight	11	Align at the top
5	Border colour	12	Align in the centre
6	Outside borders	13	Align at the bottom
7	Fill colour		

Clipboard toolbar

| 1 | Copy | 3 | Empty the clipboard |
| 2 | Paste all | 4 | Contents of the clipboard |

TOOLBARS

Picture toolbar

1... ...12

1	Insert a picture from a file	7	Crop
2	Picture control	8	Line style
3	Increase contrast	9	Recolour picture
4	Decrease contrast	10	Format picture
5	Increase brightness	11	Transparent
6	Decrease brightness	12	Restore picture

WordArt toolbar

1... ...10

1	Insert WordArt object	6	Free rotate
2	Edit WordArt text	7	Same letter heights
3	Gallery of WordArt effects	8	Vertical text
4	Format WordArt object	9	Alignment
5	WordArt shapes (text envelopes)	10	Character spacing

Shadow Settings toolbar

1... ...6

1	Show/hide shadow	4	Move shadow left
2	Move shadow up	5	Move shadow right
3	Move shadow down	6	Shadow colour

3-D Settings toolbar

1... ...10

1	3-D/2-D	6	Depth
2	Flip downwards	7	Orientation
3	Flip upwards	8	Lighting
4	Flip left	9	Surface
5	Flip right	10	3-D colour

Master toolbar

1...   ...2

1   Slide miniature   2   Close

Handout Master toolbar

1...   ...6

1   Show 2 slides per page   4   Show 6 slides per page
2   Show 3 slides per page   5   Show 9 slides per page
3   Show 4 slides per page   6   Show the outline

Animation Effects toolbar

1...   ...13

1   Animate the title   7   Laser text effect
2   Animate the slide body text   8   Typewriter text effect
3   Drive-in effect   9   Reverse text order effect
4   Flying effect   10   Drop-in text effect
5   Camera effect   11   Animation order
6   Flash once   12   Custom animation
                                   13   Animation preview

MS Graph 2000 Standard toolbar

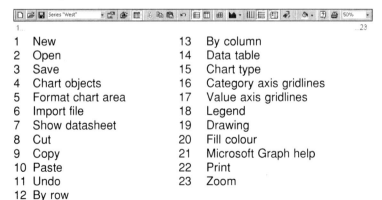

1...   ...23

1   New   13   By column
2   Open   14   Data table
3   Save   15   Chart type
4   Chart objects   16   Category axis gridlines
5   Format chart area   17   Value axis gridlines
6   Import file   18   Legend
7   Show datasheet   19   Drawing
8   Cut   20   Fill colour
9   Copy   21   Microsoft Graph help
10   Paste   22   Print
11   Undo   23   Zoom
12   By row

TOOLBARS

MS Graph 2000 Formatting toolbar

1... ...15

1	Font	9	Currency
2	Font size	10	Percentage style
3	Bold	11	Comma style
4	Italics	12	Add a decimal place
5	Underline	13	Remove a decimal place
6	Align-left	14	Orient text downwards
7	Center	15	Orient text upwards
8	Align-right		

Reviewing toolbar

1... ...7

1	Insert a comment	6	Create a task in Microsoft
2	Show/hide comments		Outlook
3	Previous comment	7	Send to mail recipient
4	Next comment		(as attachment)
5	Delete comment		

INDEX BY SUBJECT

D

DATASHEET

DELETING

DRAWING

E

E-MAIL

EFFECTS

ENVIRONMENT

F

FINDING

FONT

FORMATTING

G

GUIDES

H

HANDOUTS

HELP

HIDING

I

INSERTING

M

N

O

INDEX BY SUBJECT

INDEX BY SUBJECT

Microsoft PowerPoint 2000

Publishing

▲ **Quick Reference Guide**
▲ **User Manual**
▲ **Practical Guide**
▲ **Training CD-ROM**
▲ **Microsoft®**
   Approved Publication

VISIT OUR WEB SITE

http://www.editions-eni.com

Ask for our free brochure

For more information on our new titles please complete this card and return

Name: ....
....
Company: ....
Address: ....
....
Postcode: ....
Town: ....
Phone: ....
E-mail: ....

ENI Publishing LTD

500 Chiswick High Road

London W4 5RG